# "So Good...
# Make You Slap Your Mama!"

*by Marlyn Monette*

Enjoy!
Marlyn Monette

www.slapyourmama.com

ISBN 0-9673339-0-3

First Printing
3,000 copies printed — April 1999

Second Printing
3,000 copies printed — September 1999

Third Printing
2,000 copies printed — September 2002

# Dedication

Dedication

This cookbook is for my family — my Mom, my children, and my husband — but most of all it is for my Mom.

My Mom, Mildred Jumel White is one of those folks who says, "It's so good to see you" and means it! She truly loves people! At 95 years of age, Mom has been around for most of the 20th Century. That's a long time! The years have been good to Mom, largely due to the fact that she always wears a "happy face", expecting good things to happen each and every day.

Mom was the first resident to occupy an apartment at the beautiful Glen Retirement Village in South Shreveport when it opened in 1986. She has since moved down the hall to full care, but wherever Mom resides, she is sure to win the heart of everyone. Mom's physical health is perfect, but her memory retention is frail and she is sometimes confused; however, her social attributes and love for everyone far outweigh any deficiencies she may suffer.

Mom is, and has always been, the epitome of a Southern Belle — sort of like Aunt Pittypat in *Gone With The Wind*, having the "vapors" on a regular basis throughout my childhood. Dad carried smelling salts to family gatherings where Mom was sure to have a "weak" spell. My brother Scotty and I would vigorously fan her while everyone looked on! Mom's second favorite spot for the vapors was in church and it became sort of a religious experience for me, watching the usher carrying Mother down the aisle, with me following along behind, swinging her purse and trying to look nonchalant.

This dear lady may have been weak in some areas, but when it came to mothering and nurturing, she was the best. The one place she never had the vapors was in her kitchen; no mere weak spell could deter her when she was busily preparing the scrumptious meals that we enjoyed so much. Mom fed us food that was definitely on the Seven Basic Food Group chart and probably wasn't even aware of it. We had home grown vegetables — mustard greens, okra, tomatoes, snap beans, corn, squash — from Dad's garden with only the slightest embellishments to enhance the natural flavors. That gal could whip up the best gumbo you ever sampled! Her rice dressing and potato salad (featured), handed down by generations of Jumels, were absolutely divine, but her real masterpiece was her French

Daube and Spaghetti (featured). My brother's and my friends loved to "casually" drop by when Mom was making her famous spaghetti, knowing she would be sure to say, "Pull up a chair and join us."

Mom came by her graciousness quite naturally. She comes from a wonderful home where hospitality was the order of the day. I'm proud to say that Mom's family had a little to do with the State's development. Mother kept us enthralled as children, telling us amazing stories of her family history. Her paternal grandfather, General Allen Jumel, served as Adjutant General of Louisiana, as well as Senator, and was one of the landowners instrumental in the founding of the Leper Colony at Carville, Louisiana, donating a portion of his plantation, Point Clear, for that purpose in 1894. I have treasures of old newspaper clippings about this remarkable old man, who also attended Centenary College in Jackson, Louisiana, its place of origin.

When her grandkids came on the scene, Mom jumped into that role with relish, reading to them for hours, babysitting them for me; they simply adored her. Now, it's the great-grandchildren who talk about their "Me Me". Recently I took two of the little ones out to visit with her. She was in the hall visiting with another elderly lady when she spotted us. Her friend said, "Mildred, who are these people?" As the little ones ran into her open arms, Mom replied, "I don't know, but I think they're kin to me!"

Mom has been a widow since age 57 when my wonderful Dad, Walter Scott White, died suddenly of a heart attack. That's when we began to see the strength in that little woman; underneath all the "Aunt Pittypat" was a strong gal indeed. At age 68 she took ballroom dancing lessons with two of her sisters and learned to dance like a pro. At 92, she still does a neat jitterbug with my husband Ed, whom she adores. Ed calls her "Monkey" (and gets away with it).

In closing this dedication, I want to say, "Mom, I thank you for the stability in my life, for giving me pride, for warmth and laughter, for precious memories, for discipline, and most of all, for unconditional love. You gave to me a strong love of family and tradition, both precious gifts. I have carried your gentle voice and your soothing touch with me all of my life. Whatever I am is because of you and I am so proud to say, "there's my Mom!"

# Acknowledgments

This book would be incomplete if I fail to
acknowledge my old friend and cooking mate,
Nel Chavanne with whom I shared many wonderful times.

1939 - 1996

For the endless hours spent in proofing this book, I want to say thanks to
my husband, Edwin, and to my special friend, Beverly Pierce, who went
far beyond the call of duty. Bev had the coffee hot in the mornings and the
wine chilled in the evenings through those long hours of tedious work.
The final proofing of the completed book was done by long-time friend,
Ann May, who walked into my home one Saturday and had the nerve to
ask, "Marlyn, can I do anything to help?" And she did!! Thanks Ann!

Acknowledgments: x

# Table of Contents

# Table of Contents

# Introduction

Very few cookbooks are written in a narrative style, with stories relating to the origin of the special recipes that are being shared. I know that if I merely record ingredients and instructions, I am letting years and years of family tradition go by the wayside. These are my treasures, my secrets, and in sharing them with you, I am sharing a lifetime of memories — memories of childhood and Mom, of my children, Debbie, Donna, and Danny, and memories of the last twenty years with my husband Ed.

I am proud of my Southern heritage. With each generation we receive new life and new ideas and that is good, but the old must remain a vital part of our lives. There is no substitute for tradition; it must be respected as you would respect anything that is ageless. A passion for good food and gracious living is part of my upbringing; it is responsible for every good meal that I create and for every friend that I welcome into my home.

Since I have had many questions about the unlikely title of this cookbook, *"So Good...Make You Slap Your Mama!"*, which is also the name of my column in *Portfolio Magazine*, I would like to stress that this is simply an old South Louisiana phrase and in no way suggests any disrespect for mothers. Mamas are never, ever slapped in our genteel South!! On the contrary, "So Good...Make You Slap Your Mama" is simply a pat on the back for mama for creating a dish or a meal that is out-of-this-world delicious!

In the South Louisiana home where I grew up, our kitchen was a friendly retreat where everyone gathered to be comforted, protected, and sometimes scolded. My Mom drew people like a magnet, lavishing love and attention on everyone. Many confidences flowed between family and friends as we talked and watched Mom busily preparing meals. It wasn't until later as a young bride, armed with a set of shiny Revere Ware pots and a *Better Homes and Garden Cookbook* that I realized cooking was a little more complicated than I had believed. After several disastrous meals, I realized that I should have paid more attention to what Mom had been doing in the kitchen all those years. If anyone had told me that someday I would be a professional caterer, I would have had a good laugh. Finally, I did learn to cook — and to love it.

My repertoire of recipes includes simple family fare, as well as elegant food for entertaining. These recipes have not been tested by experts, nor have I traveled abroad to study the fine art of cooking, but I promise you they are "tried and true". It is my hope that you will find in this book some humor, as well as ideas, topped with practical advice on cooking and entertaining.

Since my book is dedicated to my family I have included a Memory Chapter, filled with pictures of family. Research for this chapter meant perusing photo albums and boxes of pictures, both new and old; what a wonderful stroll I had down memory lane. What a dilemma it was choosing which pictures to use!

Letting go of this book was difficult for me — akin to watching a child leave home for the first time without me. In gathering my material for this cookbook, I was astounded by the number of recipes which are creations of my husband Ed. Gosh, this guy could have written his own cookbook!

My hope is that as you browse through the pages of *"So Good...Make You Slap Your Mama!"* and sample some of my treasures, you will experience my passion for food, taste my traditions, and feast on my memories. Simply stated, this book is *me* and where I come from.


For all that has been, THANKS!
For all that will be, YES!
*Dag Hammarskjold*
    from his book *Markings*.

*Justin Daniel Herpin*

# *Appetizers*

Memorable occasions are more than just food. It's the little extras that make guests feel welcome. When you are hosting a party, planning is the key, with the bottom line being "make ahead". Entertaining in your home should be anticipated with pleasure and excitement, not as a chore.

Choose appetizers that achieve balance, varying color, texture, and temperature, where elegance and simplicity go hand-in-hand. Dips and molds are simple to prepare and can be made ahead, while canapes require more time. Canapes are ideal for the hostess with limited table space, as they can be passed. If you're hosting a dinner party, canapes are ideal since they allow you to limit the amount of appetizers consumed, thus insuring that your guests won't be over-stuffed when they sit down to your meal.

It is important to stick with appetizers that are not messy, and to keep *finger* food just that — *finger* food. Serve appetizers that require no more than a toothpick on the plate. If you have ever observed a guest doing a balancing act with plate, fork, and drink, you'll agree it's not a pretty sight.

When bringing appetizers to a party, stick with *cool and simple*. The guest who brings trays of canapes to bake in my kitchen at the last minute is not appreciated, especially when it's 100 degrees in the shade. *Cool and simple* will wait for you and your guests, can be made in advance, and can be interspersed with fancier creations.

For your next gathering, focus your energy on preparing ahead so that on the night of your event as you greet your guests, you will be relaxed and confident, truly ready to enjoy every moment of your special occasion. Remember, festive, not fussy!

# BRIE EN CROUTE

1 pkg. frozen puff pastry sheets
2 (6 ounce) Brie cheese rounds
¼ cup apricot preserves

¼ cup chopped pecans
1 egg yolk, lightly beaten

Unfold one sheet of puff pastry and place one brie in the center. Cover top of brie with one-half apricot preserves and one-half chopped pecans Gather the edges of the dough over the cheese to resemble a paper bag. Tie "bag" with cotton twine. Repeat procedure with the remaining pastry, brie, preserves and pecans. Place on lightly greased cookie sheet; chill one hour. Brush dough with egg yolk and bake in preheated 375 degree oven for 25 to 30 minutes; pastry will be puffed and golden. Cool for one hour before cutting into pie shaped wedges. Serve with crackers.

Yield: 15-25 servings

# CAMEMBERT PECAN DELICACY

*Simple to prepare, elegant to present — can be popped in oven right before serving.*

1 (16 ounce) Camembert cheese
½ cup dark brown sugar

3 teaspoons dry sherry
1 cup pecan halves

Scrape top of camembert to within ¼" of edges. Place on serving plate. Mix brown sugar with sherry and spread over cheese. Top with pecan halves to resemble a pie. Bake in 325 degree oven about 15 minutes, just until cheese is softened and topping is hot. Serve with your favorite crackers.

Yield: 20 servings

*When serving cheeses, it's a matter of preference;*
*brie, camembert and other soft white cheeses*
*can be substituted according to your personal taste.*

# CHEESE LOG

*This spicy log is just what the doctor ordered to get guests in the party mood! Cut log into three sections for gift-giving and wrap in festive paper and ribbon.*

2 pounds Velveeta
1 pound Velveeta, Mexican or hot
12 ounces softened cream cheese
¾ cup green onion tops, chopped
2 tablespoons seeded jalapeno pepper, chopped
¾ cup chopped pecans
½ cup bell pepper, chopped

Blend together (with hands) both Velveeta cheeses and place on waxed paper. Roll out thin into a large rectangle. Place in refrigerator to firm up while mixing remaining ingredients. For filling, mix together the cream cheese, pecans, jalapeno pepper, green onions and bell pepper. Remove cheese rectangle from refrigerator and spread filling over it. Beginning at long side, roll up, jellyroll fashion. Cut roll into two or three sections, wrap in plastic wrap and refrigerate. Freezes beautifully.

Yield: 60 servings

# PINEAPPLE CHEESE BALL

*This unique cheese ball is light and tropical — wonderful for patio parties!*

16 ounces cream cheese
1 (8½ ounce) can crushed pineapple, drained
1 teaspoon seasoned salt
2 tablespoons onion, chopped
¼ cup bell pepper, chopped
1 cup chopped pecans, divided

Mix all ingredients, reserving half of pecans for topping. Shape into a ball and roll in reserved chopped pecans; refrigerate. Serve with your favorite crackers.

Yield: 30-40 servings

## VEGETABLE CHEESE BALL

*For autumn parties, shape into two "pinecones" and shiplap with whole almonds, placing a small pine branch at the ends. Serve with fruit and assorted crackers.*

3 (8 ounce) pkgs. cream cheese
1 bunch green onion tops,
   finely chopped
1 small can chopped ripe olives,
   drained

1 small can chopped
   mushrooms, drained
1 small can chopped pimento
1 small jar chipped dried beef,
   shredded

Blend all ingredients together, form into desired shape and serve with wheat crackers.

Yield: 50-60 servings

## CHEESE PILLOWS

*This appetizer takes time and patience to prepare, but is well worth the effort. Rave reviews are guaranteed! If you're looking for "different and delicious", this is it!*

1 large loaf French bread
2 sticks margarine
½ cup shredded mozzarella
½ cup shredded sharp cheddar
½ cup shredded Swiss

6 ounces cream cheese
1 teaspoon dry mustard
¼ teaspoon black pepper
½ teaspoon salt
4 egg whites, beaten until stiff

Remove crust from bread and cut into 1" cubes; set aside. Melt margarine and add remaining ingredients except egg whites. Use a wire whisk to blend well. When well blended, fold in egg whites. With tongs, dip bread squares, one at a time, into cheese mixture and place untouching on a cookie sheet. Flash freeze. When frozen, place in a ziplock bag and store in freezer until ready to bake. To bake: place frozen squares on a cookie sheet and bake in preheated 400 degree oven for 10-15 minutes.

Yield: 45-50 squares

## DAWN'S CHEESE KRISPIES

*My special friend Dawn Barnett, a marvelous cook who can make a mudpie taste succulent, shared this recipe with me when I declared that I "hate to make those time-consuming Cheese Straws." These are simple to make and the cereal adds pizzazz!*

2 sticks butter
10 ounces sharp cheddar, grated
2 cups flour

1 pinch salt
Dash Cayenne pepper
2 cups Rice Krispies cereal

Cream butter and grated cheese. Add flour, salt and pepper; add cereal. Roll into 1-inch balls and place on baking sheet. Press with the back of a fork to flatten. Bake in 275 degree oven for 20 to 30 minutes. Do not overbake. Sprinkle lightly with pepper.

Yield: 6 dozen


## DONNA'S ARTICHOKE/SPINACH DIP

*On a recent visit to my daughter Donna's home, she prepared this delicious dip. Slim, trim Donna swears she can eat it all by herself. After tasting it, I understand why — it is divine!*

1 (9 ounce) frozen creamed
  spinach, thawed
¾ cup grated Parmesan
  (reserve ¼ cup for topping)
½ teaspoon white pepper

1 (14 ounce) can artichoke hearts,
  drained and chopped
1 teaspoon fresh lemon juice
1 cup mozzarella cheese,
  shredded

Combine all ingredients and blend well. Place in sprayed baking dish. Top with reserved Parmesan cheese. Bake in 350 degree oven until hot and bubbly, about 20 minutes. Serve with your favorite crackers. This dish also makes a wonderful casserole with a meal.

Yield: 15 servings

*A block of cream cheese topped with pepper jelly
provides a great snack for drop-in guests.*

## FESTIVE CORN DIP

*This dip is making the rounds! I received four variations from readers of my food column — all were delicious. This one is a winner, for either a ladies luncheon served on lettuce or as a dip for cocktail parties.*

2 cups corn, drained
1 cup sour cream
1 cup Hellmann's mayonnaise
1 small can chopped green chilis
½ cup chopped green onion tops
1 deseeded jalapeno pepper,
   chopped

1 small jar chopped pimentos,
   drained
¼ cup chopped bell pepper
4 ounces shredded cheddar cheese
4 ounces shredded Monterrey
   Jack cheese, with peppers
2 pounds boiled shrimp or crawfish

Mix all ingredients until well blended. Serve with corn chips or on lettuce for luncheons.
Yield: Dip: 40 servings   Salad: 6-8 servings

## LIGHT SHRIMP DIP/SALAD

*This delicious dip/salad is the answer to a dieter's prayers! With crackers or corn chips for a cocktail party, or as a perfect luncheon offering, this light, tasty dish will become a favorite. Don't let the cottage cheese throw you; it truly complements the dish.*

½ cup bell pepper, chopped
½ cup celery, chopped
½ cup radishes, chopped
½ cup green onions, chopped
½ cup sharp cheddar, grated
Salt and black pepper, to taste

3 tablespoons sweet pickle
   relish, drained
1 cup small curd cottage cheese
3 pounds spicy boiled shrimp,
   chopped
4 heaping tablespoons prepared
   French onion dip

Toss all ingredients, except French onion dip. Blend in French onion dip; refrigerate.
Yield: Dip: 15-20 servings   Salad: 4-6 servings

# SPINACH DIP

*No cookbook is complete without a spinach dip. After trying many varieties, I found the addition of bacon and horseradish made this one an instant hit with guests!*

3 pkgs. frozen, chopped spinach,
   squeezed very dry
1 cup Hellmann's mayonnaise
½ cup green onion tops, chopped
½ cup fried bacon, crumbled
½ cup water chestnuts, chopped

¼ cup grated Parmesan
Cayenne pepper, to taste
Salt, to taste
Garlic powder, to taste
1 teaspoon creamed horseradish
   (or more to suit taste)

Blend together all ingredients. For presentation, place in hollowed out round white or rye bread. Serve with wheat crackers or a round sweet cracker.

Yield: 30-40 servings

# ARTICHOKE/CHEESE SNACK

*This layered appetizer is easy, delectable, and can be made a day ahead.*

1 large can water packed artichoke
   hearts, drained, cut in quarters
2 jars marinated artichokes,
   drained, cut in quarters

1 (4 ounce) can chopped green
   chilis, drained
8-10 tablespoons Hellmann's
   mayonnaise
½ pound Velveeta, grated

In a 13x9x2" glass baking dish or hollowed out French bread, layer the ingredients in the order listed, finishing with Velveeta. Bake in 325 degree oven until hot and bubbly.

Yield: 15-20 servings

## ZESTY TAMALE DIP

*There is nothing gourmet about this dip, but it is delicious and always seems to disappear rapidly. Served piping hot in a chafer, along with corn chips or tortillas, it is a hearty favorite, especially with the guys.*

2 (15 ounce) cans hot tamales
2 (15 ounce) cans chili, no beans
1 pound grated cheddar cheese
2 medium onions, chopped fine

1 can diced chilies
1 tablespoon garlic puree
Dash of Tabasco and chili powder
1 jalapeno, chopped, deseeded

Drain tamales, remove shucks. Mash tamales well and blend together with remaining ingredients. Heat over low temperature, stirring frequently. Serve hot in chafer, with additional grated cheese on top.

Yield: 35-40 servings

## PLAIN OLE HAMBURGER DIP

*Another tried and true appetizer, especially for a teenage party.*

1½ pounds ground chuck
1 medium onion, chopped
½ pound fresh, sliced mushrooms
1 small can diced green chilies

1 (10 ounce) can Ro-tel tomatoes
8 ounces Jalapeno cheese
8 ounces Velveeta

In a heavy skillet, cook ground chuck, onions and mushrooms until done. Drain off all grease. Add Ro-tel, green chilies and shredded cheeses. Stir until all cheese melts. Serve hot in a chafer with your favorite chips or toast rounds.

Yield: 15-20 servings

# BACON-CHEESE RING

*The combination of cheese, onion and bacon make this a party hit. Present with seasonal fruit, along with the strawberry preserves for that added dollop of flavor. This cheese ring freezes beautifully.*

2 ounces Hormel <u>real</u> bacon pieces
2 pounds sharp Cheddar, grated
½ bunch green onion tops,
   finely chopped

1 cup Hellmann's mayonnaise
1½ teaspoons cayenne pepper
1 cup chopped roasted pecans
²/₃ cup strawberry preserves

Allow cheese to soften and combine all ingredients, except strawberry preserves — blend well. Press cheese mixture firmly into a six-cup ring mold. Refrigerate until firm. Unmold onto serving tray and garnish with fresh fruit. Place a small bowl in center of mold and spoon in strawberry preserves. Serve with assorted crackers.
Yield: 35-40 servings

# PARTY SHRIMP WITH PIZZAZZ

8 pounds spicy boiled, peeled
   medium sized shrimp
²/₃ cup chopped green onion tops

SAUCE:
3 ripe, mashed avocados
²/₃ cup lemon juice
¼ cup creole mustard
2 tablespoons Worcestershire

1 pound fresh whole mushrooms
1 cup celery, chopped
4 small jars marinated
   artichoke hearts (optional)

5 tablespoons horseradish
½ cup vegetable oil
1 tablespoon crushed garlic
⅛ teaspoon red pepper flakes

Combine shrimp, celery, mushrooms, onions and artichoke hearts. Combine sauce ingredients and toss well with shrimp mixture. Chill. (Serve on curly lettuce, garnished with ripe olives, yellow bell pepper rings and cherry tomatoes).
Yield: Appetizer: 30 servings    Luncheon: 10-12 servings

# SHRIMP DIP

*Shrimp dips take time to prepare if you're using the old fashioned way, which begins with raw, fresh shrimp and boiling and peeling them. It's worth it when you taste the flavor.*

8 ounces cream cheese
8-10 green onion tops, chopped
1 tablespoon lemon juice
Scant mayonnaise, to blend
Scant salt, to taste

2 dashes Tabasco
1 tablespoon Worcestershire
2 pounds spicy boiled, coarsely
    chopped shrimp

Allow cream cheese to soften and combine with all remaining ingredients, folding in shrimp last. This is best made a day ahead to let flavors blend. Serve with large corn chips.
Yield: 15-20 servings

# MARINATED SHRIMP

10 pounds boiled, peeled shrimp
1 pound fresh mushrooms
1 quart olive oil
1½ cups garlic vinegar
1½ cups dry sherry
1-2 teaspoons salt
1 teaspoon sugar

Cayenne pepper, to taste
2 lemons, sliced
6 onions, thinly sliced
1 tablespoon Tony Chachere's
    seasoning
1 tablespoon Tabasco

Layer mushrooms and shrimp in a flat dish. Mix next six ingredients and pour over shrimp and mushrooms, adding lemon slices. Cover and refrigerate for three days, stirring at intervals. Add onions and adjust seasonings 24 hours before serving.
Yield: 18 servings

*When boiling shrimp add sugar to the water for more flavor.*

# HEAVENLY REMOULADE SAUCE

*Set a beautiful cocktail table with a cut glass bowl lined with lettuce, filled with zesty boiled shrimp and topped with Heavenly Remoulade Sauce. Garnish with chunks of hard-boiled egg and fresh tomato for color. I have tried many remoulade sauces in my life, but this is the winner hands down. I must give credit for this exotic dish to my dear friend Henry Poulsen, a true gourmet cook. When we dine at the beautiful home of Henry and his multi-talented wife LaMuriel, we are always assured of a unique, succulent gourmet meal, not to mention excellent company.*

1 cup Hellmann's mayonnaise
½ cup olive oil
½ cup bottled French dressing
1 tablespoon anchovy paste
Juice of 1 lemon
2 teaspoons coarse ground
    black pepper
3 hard-boiled eggs, finely chopped

1 teaspoon Worcestershire
1 teaspoon dry mustard
2 tablespoons red wine vinegar
1 tablespoon tarragon vinegar
4 tablespoons chopped capers
1 tablespoon bottled onion juice
2 teaspoons pureed garlic

With whisk, blend together the first five ingredients and cover with coarse black pepper. Add remaining ingredients in order listed and mix well. Serve with fresh boiled shrimp or on lump crab meat. Magnifique!

Yield: 2 cups (approximately)

*When serving Shrimp Remoulade at a party,*
*add medium sized fresh mushrooms to the party tray.*
*It's amazing how wonderful mushrooms taste in remoulade sauce!*
*This serves as a filler, as well as a delicious taste treat.*

## SHRIMP IN PUFF PASTRY

*For the small dinner party in your home, this golden puff pastry, filled with a harmony of flavors — creamy cheese, zesty shrimp and horseradish — delights guests.*

8 ounces softened cream cheese
1 pound boiled, chopped shrimp
2 teaspoons horseradish
¼ teaspoon Tabasco
Scant salt and black pepper

1 sheet frozen, puff pastry
   sheet, thawed
1 tablespoon milk
¼ cup freshly grated
   Parmesan or Romano

Mix first five ingredients. Roll out puff pastry sheet on floured circle into a 16" x 18" rectangle. Spread filling lengthwise over 14" x 16" area of pastry. Carefully transfer pastry sheet onto a baking sheet that's been sprayed with cooking spray. Brush edges of pastry sheet with milk and overlap, covering filling. Brush top with remaining milk and sprinkle with Parmesan. Bake in 400 degree oven for 25-30 minutes until puff pastry is golden. Cool slightly and slice into serving pieces.

Yield: 15-20 servings

## HOT CRABMEAT DIP

2 (8 ounce) pkgs. cream cheese
½ cup horseradish
½ cup green onion tops, chopped

½ pound lump crabmeat
½ cup sliced almonds
Paprika, to taste

Mix together cream cheese, horseradish and green onions; fold in crabmeat. Spread mixture in a baking dish. Top with almonds and sprinkle with paprika. Bake uncovered in 375 degree oven for 20 minutes. Serve with assorted crackers.

Yield: 20 servings

Variation: Place in hollowed out French bread — bake and serve.

# OYSTER ROLL

2 (8 ounce) pkgs. cream cheese
2 cans smoked oysters, drained
2 teaspoons Worcestershire
Crushed garlic to taste

½ small onion, minced fine
2-3 tablespoons Hellmann's
   mayonnaise
Salt, to taste

Blend just enough mayonnaise into cream cheese to make it spreadable. Add Worcestershire sauce, garlic, onion and salt. Combine well. Spread mixture out to about ½ inch thickness on waxed paper. Chop smoked oysters and spread them on top of cheese mixture. At this point, carefully place in refrigerator for about 15 minutes to firm up mixture. Remove from refrigerator and roll as a jelly roll, using a knife to get started. Chill for 24 hours. Serve with toastpoints or crackers.

Yield: 30-35 servings

# GLORIOUS CRAB/PHILLY

*This treat can be "dressed up" in a fancy mold for a cocktail party, or served plain for drop-in guests. The ingredients are simple, but it is important to use good quality crabmeat. For a party I shape the cream cheese into a shallow fish-shaped mold. Comments are "What is in this divine mold?" The best news is, you don't have to be Betty Crocker to make it! This would also be great with Heavenly Remoulade Sauce!*

2 (8 ounce) cream cheese
1 bottle Heinz Cocktail Sauce
   or your own homemade sauce

1 (6 ounce) can lump crabmeat or
   ½ pound fresh crabmeat
½ cup green onion tops, chopped

Place blocks of cream cheese touching, side-by-side, on a serving plate. Cover with picked, drained crabmeat and pour cocktail sauce over the top. Sprinkle with chopped green onions. Serve with crackers of your choice.

Yield: 15-20 servings

# SHRIMP/ASPARAGUS CREATION

*The idea for this dish came from my hairstylist, Sandy Toney who is not only a magician with hair, but a gourmet cook as well. While experimenting with it, I served it to guests often in a short period of time — both as an appetizer and as a first course to dinner. After the fourth serving, I asked my husband how he liked it. He replied, "I savored it the first and second time, enjoyed it the third, and frankly Marlyn, I tolerated it last night!" I guess I did "overkill", but what counts is that the guests LOVED it! The marriage of these flavors and textures is truly wonderful and it can be made hours ahead!*

4-5 large slices thin sliced ham,
  (not smoked)
4 ounces Monterrey Jack cheese
  or other mild white cheese,
  cut in slivers

½ pound fresh asparagus,
  steamed one minute and
  cut in 2-inch pieces
1 pound large, well-seasoned
  boiled shrimp

Scampi Sauce:
1 stick BUTTER
Juice of one lemon

1½ tablespoons crushed garlic
¼ cup dry white wine

Cut ham lengthwise into ¼ inch strips. Combine 1 shrimp, 1 piece asparagus, 1 sliver cheese and wrap firmly with 1 strip ham. Secure with toothpick and place in shallow baking dish. Repeat procedure, using all remaining ingredients. Prepare Scampi Sauce by melting butter in saucepan and blending in remaining ingredients. Drizzle Scampi Sauce over wrapped appetizers in baking dish. Let sit to marinate until ready to serve. When ready to serve, place under broiler and broil quickly — only until hot. Serve immediately.

Yield: 20-25 appetizers (approximately)

Tip: As a first course, wrap appetizers and place in individual dishes, with no toothpicks; drizzle with sauce and broil. Serve with French bread for "sopping" up the Scampi Sauce.

*Keep the toothpicks plain;*
*your food is the focal point,*
*not a fuchsia cellophane-frilled toothpick!*

# ROLLUPS

*This popular snack has been around since the early '80's. I first sampled them while on a boating trip with the Shreveport Power Squadron. Our "Captains" may be in charge at the helm of the boat, but we "1st Mates" keep things in hand when it comes to preparing delicious food for dining and snacking on the water. We find that Rollups keep well for several days in the ice chest. They are also easy to prepare, although I am sad to say that in the last few years there's been a change in the flour tortilla — they all now seem to be "fat-free or low-fat". While that is great for our waistlines, it makes preparing this dish something less than "simple". "Less fat" means "less moist", therefore, the tortilla tends to crack easily and makes rolling difficult. When purchasing flour tortillas, check them for flexibility, as some brands are more pliable than others. Let's face it — some things are better with a little fat!!*

3 ounces cream cheese
8 ounces sour cream
5-6 stems green onion tops
   finely chopped

Cayenne pepper, to taste
Scant salt
1 package medium-sized
   flour tortillas

Blend cream cheese, sour cream and green onion tops until smooth and easy to spread. With knife, spread mixture on flour tortillas liberally. Roll up tortilla, being careful to roll "tight" when you start so there's no hole in the center. Stack on a cookie sheet and place in refrigerator for six hours, preferably overnight. Cut into 1-inch pieces and store in airtight container. Keeps well in refrigerator for one week. Serve with Picante Sauce for dipping.
Yield: 50-60 snacks

*Good rule of thumb:*
*If you can't pick it up, don't eat it!*
*(Miss Piggy)*

# ALMOND-HAM ROLLUPS

*These rollups are a perfect complement to your heavier appetizers for a party. The slight crunch of the almonds is a mystery to guests — everyone wants to know what's in them.*

8 ounces softened cream cheese
2 tablespoons Hellmann's
    mayonnaise
2 teaspoons finely minced onion
1 teaspoon Worcestershire
½ teaspoon dry mustard

¼ teaspoon each: paprika,
    cayenne pepper, Tabasco
1 tablespoon toasted almonds,
    finely chopped
1 pound thinly sliced boiled ham

Combine all ingredients except ham, stirring until blended. Spread 1 tablespoon mixture on each ham slice. Roll up jellyroll fashion, starting at short end. Place in airtight container to retain moisture (may be frozen at this point). To serve, cut each roll into ¾ inch slices. Serve with toothpicks. Freezes well for a short period of time.

Yield: 5 dozen

# HAM/OLIVE ROLLUPS

1 pkg. medium flour tortillas
12 slices thinly sliced ham
8 ounces cream cheese

½ cup chopped, drained green
    olives w/pimentos
Cayenne pepper, to taste

Place slice of ham on tortilla. Spread cream cheese evenly on ham. Sprinkle lightly with cayenne pepper, then with chopped olives. Roll tightly. Chill for several hours and slice to ¾ inch size. Serve with toothpicks.

Yield: 50 rollups

Variation: Substitute 1 crispy, steamed fresh asparagus spear for the olives — place on ham slice and roll. For ease in preparation, well-drained canned asparagus can be used.

## ARTICHOKE TOAST
*Simple, simple, simple — and so delectable!*

1 (6 ounce) jar marinated
   artichoke hearts, chopped
1 cup Hellmann's mayonnaise
6 ounces grated Parmesan cheese,
   preferably fresh

½ cup green onion tops, chopped
Dash Tabasco, to taste
Cayenne pepper, to taste
1 package cocktail sized sour
   dough bread

Mix all ingredients together, blending well. Spread liberally on bread rounds. (Can be placed on cookie sheets and frozen at this point. Drop in plastic bags and return to freezer until ready to bake.) Place desired amount of toasts on cookie sheet and bake in 375 degree oven for 10-15 minutes, until bread is crisp and topping is hot and bubbly.

Yield: 50 (approximately)

## STUFFED CHERRY TOMATOES
*Stuffing these tiny gems is not fun, but they are colorful and lend a festive aura to your vegetable tray. The combination of horseradish and bacon is a sure winner!*

2 dozen cherry tomatoes
8 ounces softened cream cheese

2 tablespoons horseradish
½ cup crumbled lean bacon

Cut top off each tomato. Carefully scoop out pulp and invert on paper towels to drain. Mix remaining ingredients well and spoon or pipe into tomato shells. Chill until serving.

Yield: 2 dozen

*At a cocktail party one evening a dignified elderly lady,
dressed to the nines in an elegant black cocktail gown, was
sprayed with tomato seeds when another guest eagerly bit into
a plump red cherry tomato. Cherry tomatoes can be tricky!*

## JALAPENO FUDGE

*Served with fried fish, Mexican food, or as an appetizer, Jalapeno Fudge is a popular item in the south. The original recipe consisted of only cheddar, eggs, and jalapenos. To add color to party trays, I added Monterrey Jack cheese and pimento.*

1 pound grated Monterrey
   Jack cheese
1½ cups chopped seedless
   jalapeno peppers

1 pound sharp cheddar, grated
5-6 eggs, well beaten
1 teaspoon nutmeg
1 small jar chopped pimento

Lightly spray 13x9x2 inch Pyrex dish. Layer as follows: Monterrey Jack, jalapenos, sharp cheddar. Beat eggs with nutmeg and pour carefully over all layers; press down firmly to pack. Sprinkle with drained pimento for color. Bake uncovered in 400 degree oven for 30-40 minutes, until eggs are set. Let sit about 20 minutes before cutting into squares.

Yield: 50 small squares

## SAUSAGE ON RYE

*This simple canape is hard to beat, therefore, I like to keep a supply in the freezer at all times. My son, Danny can "put away" a cookie sheet full of them in one sitting, as can his son Alec. They will keep for six to eight weeks if stored in airtight plastic bags.*

1 loaf Pepperidge Farm
   Party Rye Bread

1 pound ground pork sausage
1 pkg. (6 ounce) jalapeno cheese

Fry sausage and drain well. (A black iron skillet will absorb most of the grease.) Add jalapeno cheese and stir until melted. Pat this mixture with paper towels to absorb grease from cheese. Spread on Party Rye bread slices and place on cookie sheet. (Can flash freeze at this point) To serve, place desired amount of bread rounds on a cookie sheet and bake in 375 degree oven for 15 minutes or until bread is crisp and topping is piping hot.

Yield: 35-40

# STUFFED MUSHROOMS

*There are many varieties of stuffed mushrooms — this one's our favorite. Crabmeat is the focal point and is unencumbered by a lot of other ingredients.*

| | |
|---|---|
| 12 large mushrooms | ½ pound lump or claw crabmeat |
| 3 stalks green onions, chopped | ½ cup Italian breadcrumbs |
| 1 tablespoon garlic puree | ¼ cup Romano cheese |
| ½ cup olive oil | 3 tablespoons dry white wine |

Remove stems from mushrooms and chop; saute with green onion and garlic in olive oil. Lightly fold in crabmeat and simmer low about 5 minutes. Pile mixture lightly in large mushroom caps and place in 13x9x2 lightly sprayed baking dish. Cover each filled mushroom with Italian breadcrumbs and Romano cheese. Drizzle wine lightly over mushrooms. Bake uncovered in 350 degree oven until hot and bubbly, about 15 minutes.

Yield: 12

# OYSTERS EN BROCHETTE

*Once a year, we treat ourselves to a gallon of fresh oysters and invite friends over. The feast begins with raw oysters and spicy cocktail sauce, washed down with ice cold beer or white wine. We then prepare En Brochette, served with hushpuppies, cheese stuffed jalapenos, and slaw. As an appetizer, En Brochette is great served hot in a chafer — just be sure you have lots of help in the kitchen because they must be served immediately.*

| | |
|---|---|
| 24 medium to large fresh oysters | Cayenne pepper, to taste |
| 12 slices lean bacon, cut in half | 24 toothpicks |
| ½ cup flour | 1½ cups cooking oil |

Wrap each oyster in ½ slice bacon and secure with a toothpick. Roll in flour that has been lightly seasoned with cayenne pepper. Place in hot cooking oil and fry quickly, until bacon is crisp. Drain well and serve. Do not overcook oysters!

Yield: 24

## SHRIMP CANAPES

*The dill pickle relish is the secret here — lends a very unique flavor!*

1 cup boiled shrimp, chopped
1 cup sharp cheddar, grated
1/3 cup Hellmann's mayonnaise
1 teaspoon onion, minced
2 tablespoons dill pickle relish

1 teaspoon Tabasco
Cayenne pepper to taste
Dash salt
1 teaspoon pureed garlic
48 sourdough party bread rounds

Combine all ingredients except bread rounds. Toast one side of bread round and spread shrimp mixture on toasted side. Bake in a 350 degree oven for 15 minutes until bread is crisp and topping is hot and bubbly.

Yield: 50

## SALMON DELIGHTS

*These tiny treats will delight guests and are especially nice for brunches. They must be assembled and served immediately so have all your ingredients lined up.*

1 (8 ounce) cream cheese
6 ounce smoked salmon or lox
1 small red onion, finely chopped

½ cup nonpareille capers
1 bag (12) miniature bagels,
   sliced in half horizontally

Place a piece of salmon on each bagel half. Top with a dollop of cream cheese. Sprinkle with red onion, then with capers. Serve immediately.

Yield: 24 canapes

*Never let guests wander around searching for a napkin.*
*When party planning, allow at least three napkins per guest.*

## BEV'S SUMMER SAUSAGE TREATS

*My special friend, Beverly Pierce, a neat lady who also happens to be a superb cook, shared this delightful treat with me. They are out-of-this-world, to-die-for, and whatever other superlatives you can think of! Thanks, Bev! The world is a better place for having you in it.*

1 pound Huses Jalapeno Cheese
   Summer Sausage (or summer
   sausage of your choice)
¼ cup light Karo syrup
Lemon pepper, to taste
Dash of Tony Chachere's seasoning

Remove all casing from the summer sausage and place it on waxed paper. Bathe lightly with light Karo syrup. Sprinkle heavily with lemon pepper seasoning and a small amount of Tony Chachere's. Place on a baking pan that has been lined with aluminum foil. Bake uncovered in a 350 degree oven for one hour. Slice thin and serve with crackers.

Yield: 25-30

## PARTY CREAM CHEESE SANDWICHES

*This party sandwich recipe has been circulating for years, but bears repeating. There are many pluses: delicious flavor, economical ingredients, and can be made ahead.*

8 ounces cream cheese, softened
½ small can chopped black olives
²/₃ cup toasted pecans,
   chopped fine
2 teaspoons milk
⅛ teaspoon garlic powder
3 stalks green onion tops,
   finely chopped
Tabasco, to taste
White pepper, to taste
1 large loaf sandwich
   bread, thin sliced

Mix together all ingredients and spread on bread slice, topping with another slice of bread. Cut off crusts, then cut into quarters. Refrigerate until serving.

Yield: 44

*Adam Shane Herpin*

# Soups

When I think of soup, I think of comfort, warmth and home! I think of a crisp fall evening, a hint of winter, times that form the perfect backdrop for a soup dinner. Soup is a meal unto itself — a staple that can be made ahead. Soup is low in cost and easy to prepare. Soups can *wait*, giving you valuable time to devote to other things. To sum it up, soups can help chase away almost anything that "ails" you. Why do you think your Mama has been making chicken soup when you're not "up to snuff" ever since you were a kid? It's therapeutic!

There are many types of soups — delicate bisques, hearty chowders, light broths, flavorful gumbos. When my children were growing up, my pantry was always filled with various canned soups, as that is all these picky creatures would eat. Any attempts at feeding them my homemade soup met with crinkled little noses! It was enough to give a Mom a complex!

These days, with hospitality taking on a more casual look, what could be more fun than a soup or gumbo party? Paired with a variety of specialty breads and a delectable salad, this is an entree that will keep guests coming back for "just another spoonful". One of our most memorable parties was a Super Bowl party in our home where the main entree was seafood gumbo, served with Caesar salad and crispy French bread. Guests served themselves South Louisiana style from the massive gumbo pot in the kitchen, filling their huge mugs with the steaming hot brew. I don't recall any party in our home that we have enjoyed more, and I think our guests would agree that a good time was had by all!

# CHICKEN AND SAUSAGE GUMBO

*No self-respecting South Louisiana gal can write a cookbook and not feature gumbo, although it is difficult to put on paper what has always been a "pinch of this and a pinch of that". I learned to cook by watching Mom and I still remember my first gumbo lesson, with Mom patiently guiding me through each step. With the gumbo simmering at last, Miss Know-It-All decided to add red peppers when Mom's back was turned. I dumped about half a can of dried red peppers into the pot of simmering gumbo and saw, to my horror, about 500 tiny black "moving" things floating on the top — at that point, I panicked and STIRRED! I learned two lessons from this: check your seasonings often and more important, MIND YOUR MAMA!*

1 (4-5 pound) hen or
   2 (3 pound) fryers, cut up
4 large onions, chopped, divided
8 stalks celery, chopped, divided
1 medium bell pepper, chopped
3 tablespoons pureed garlic
¾ cup vegetable oil
¾ cup flour
1 box frozen cut okra

2 tablespoons Creole seasoning
Cayenne pepper and salt, to taste
2 bay leaves
3 chicken bouillon cubes
1 pound smoked sausage
1 cup chopped green onion tops
½ cup parsley, chopped
Gumbo filet, to taste

Boil chicken in water seasoned with 2 onions and 4 stalks celery, salt, pepper, Creole seasoning, and cayenne pepper until tender. Reserve broth. Cool chicken and debone. In a heavy pot, heat oil, blend in flour and make a dark brown roux; add remainder of onions and celery, bell pepper, garlic and saute on low heat until vegetables are tender. Add sliced okra and simmer until slime is out. Strain broth that chicken was boiled in and add to roux and vegetables. Add Creole seasoning, cayenne, bay leaves, bouillon cubes, and other seasonings; let simmer slowly for 1½ hours. Meanwhile, cut sausage into 1-inch links and saute; drain well and add to gumbo, along with the deboned chicken. Check seasonings and simmer slowly for another hour. Before serving, add parsley and green onion tops. Place gumbo filet on table for individual serving.

Yield: 12 servings

# SEAFOOD GUMBO

*There is no fast, simple way to make good gumbo. If it's to be rich and succulent, it requires slow cooking in order for the wonderful ingredients to blend. My duck gumbo takes two days to prepare — I didn't have the energy to try to put it on paper. Anyhow, no one in their right mind would go to the trouble to make it my way.*

| | |
|---|---|
| 5 large onions, chopped | 3 bay leaves |
| 6 stalks celery, chopped | 1 tablespoon cayenne pepper |
| 2 large bell peppers, chopped | 3 tablespoons Worcestershire |
| 4 pods garlic, chopped | Salt and pepper to taste |
| 1 stick margarine | 5 pounds raw shrimp, peeled |
| ¾ cup vegetable oil | 1 pint raw oysters, drained |
| ¾ cup flour | ¾ cup chopped parsley |
| 1 can Ro-tel tomatoes | 1½ cups green onions, chopped |
| 1 box frozen chopped okra, thawed | ½ pound crabmeat, optional |

In heavy Dutch oven, saute chopped vegetables in margarine, reserving ½ cup onions. In separate heavy skillet, make a dark brown roux. When roux is brown, add tomatoes and simmer awhile; add this mixture to sauteed vegetables in Dutch oven. At that time, add about 2 cups water to this mixture and stir well. In skillet where roux was made, add okra and saute until slime is out, then add reserved ½ cup onion and cook about 10 minutes longer; add to gumbo mixture. At that point, add a "handful" of shrimp, bay leaves, salt, red pepper, Worcestershire, and about 1½ quarts water. Let this simmer on a low heat for about two to three hours, stirring occasionally. About 30 minutes before serving, add remainder of shrimp, green onions, and parsley. Add oysters and crabmeat about ten minutes before serving and cook five minutes longer. Put gumbo filet on table for individual serving.

Yield: 12-14 servings

*Since gumbo is time consuming to make,
it's wise to make large batches and freeze for future meals;
also, the flavor gets better and better.*

## BROCCOLI-CHEESE SOUP

*With all due modesty, I guarantee this is the best Broccoli Soup in the state — perhaps in the world! It is rich and flavorful — guaranteed to be a hit with your family. This soup is very gourmet when served in hollowed-out hard rolls.*

| | |
|---|---|
| 1 medium onion, chopped | 3 (12 ounce) cans evaporated milk |
| 1 stick butter | 1 (6 ounce) roll Jalapeno cheese |
| 2 cans Cream of Chicken Soup | 2 pkgs. frozen chopped broccoli |
| 1 can Cream of Mushroom Soup | Dash of nutmeg |

Saute onion in butter. Add soups and milk. Stir until well blended and add Jalapeno cheese that has been cut into cubes. Add the broccoli and nutmeg. Stir over medium heat until all ingredients are well blended and cheese is melted. Let simmer on very low heat for about 30 minutes. (Freezes well)

Yield: 6-8 servings

Tip: Velveeta, with a chopped jalapeno added can be substituted for Jalapeno cheese.

## SIMPLE SHRIMP SOUP

| | |
|---|---|
| 3 cans Cream of Mushroom Soup | Dash Tabasco |
| 2 cans milk | Dash Worcestershire |
| 1 pound peeled raw shrimp | 3 tablespoons dry sherry |
| 4 green onions, minced | Salt and pepper, to taste |
| ½ cup celery, minced | |

Mix soup and milk and heat gently until it simmers. Add remaining ingredients, except sherry, salt and pepper. Bring to a slow simmer and cook for 5-6 minutes. Add sherry, salt and pepper.

Yield: 4-6 servings

# MUSHROOM BISQUE

½ cup butter
½ pound fresh mushrooms, sliced
⅓ cup onion, chopped
1 tablespoon minced garlic
1 tablespoon fresh lemon juice
3 tablespoons flour

4 cups chicken broth
2 teaspoons salt
½ teaspoon pepper
Parsley, chopped
2 cups Half & Half
2 tablespoons dry sherry (optional)

Heat butter and saute mushrooms, onion and garlic for 10 minutes. Add lemon juice and blend in flour. Gradually add broth, salt and pepper. Cook, stirring constantly until thickened. Stir in cream and heat thoroughly. Add sherry and serve. Very attractive presentation served with thin slices of lemon.

Yield: 6 servings

# ARTICHOKE SOUP

*A simple soup — absolutely divine! This one tastes as if it's been simmering on the stove for days!*

1 medium onion, chopped
½ stick margarine
1 can Cream of Onion Soup
1 can Cream of Celery Soup
1 can artichoke hearts
    (packed in water)

1½ cans water, plus juice from
    artichoke hearts
Parsley, to taste
Thin sliced lemons

Saute onion in margarine until tender; blend in soups, using wire whisk. Add water and artichoke juice. Cut artichoke hearts into 8 pieces and add to soup. Simmer for 30 minutes on low heat. To serve, sprinkle parsley on top and float a thin slice of lemon.

Yield: 4-6 servings

Tip: Ten minutes before serving, add 1 pint drained raw oysters. Delicious!

# CLAM CHOWDER

*This wonderful, simple chowder will delight even the most discriminating palate! This soup recipe was shared by my dear friend Nel Chavanne who passed away in 1996. For many years on Christmas Eve, friends and relatives, both young and old, gathered at the Chavanne home to feast on Nel's bountiful table of food, but most of all, they gathered for her warmth and hospitality. Her Clam Chowder was everyone's favorite, and they returned again and again to refill their bowls. When I close my eyes, I can still see Nel's gleaming antique silver chafer filled to the brim with this scrumptious brew, along with a silver tray offering crispy toastpoints nearby! I hope you'll try this simple-to-make chowder; it is indeed wonderful!*

½ stick butter or margarine
2 onions, chopped
2 ribs celery, chopped
2 cans minced clams

1 (10 ounce) Cream of Celery Soup
1 soup can homogenized milk
2 red potatoes, peeled and diced
Salt, pepper, parsley, to taste

Saute the onions and celery in butter and set aside. Drain clams and reserve juice. In saucepan, combine the clam juice, sauteed onions and celery, and remaining ingredients, except clams. Simmer 30 minutes and add clams. Simmer for about one hour on very low heat. When potatoes are tender, mash some of them with a potato masher, to thicken soup. If not thick enough to your taste, let soup cook down a little more. If too thick, add a dash more milk. Sprinkle with parsley to serve. Serve piping hot with Melba, toastpoints, or crusty French bread.

Yield:  15 small servings (appetizer)    6 servings (entree)

*To add texture and flavor to a clear, homemade soup, add well beaten egg yolks. In early French cooking, this addition of egg yolk was called a "liaison."*

# OYSTER BISQUE

3 tablespoons butter
3 tablespoons flour
3 dozen oysters w/liquid
3 tablespoons chopped
  green onions

1 pint Half & Half
Salt and white pepper, to taste
Dash Tabasco
3 tablespoons dry sherry

Melt butter in sauce pan and blend in flour until smooth. Stir in chopped green onions and simmer a few minutes. Slowly add Half & Half, and heat gently, stirring constantly. When hot (but not boiling!) add salt, white pepper, Tabasco and oysters. Heat until edges of oysters curl. Add sherry and serve immediately.

Yield: 2-3 servings

# CAROL'S POTATO SOUP

*This is a light, delicious soup for you who are watching your fat and/ or cholesterol. It was passed on to me by my talented daughter-in-law, Carol. I'm so proud that Carol loves to cook — that means she's taking good care of my son, not to mention grandkids!*

4-6 russet potatoes
2 bunches green onions, chopped
2 stalks celery, chopped
1 tablespoon oil
3 carrots, sliced
1 can Ro-tel tomatoes

1 teaspoon salt
White pepper, to taste
½ cup white wine
½ cup milk
Fresh rosemary, to taste
  (optional)

Saute all vegetables in oil, except potatoes. Add Ro-tel tomatoes, salt, white pepper, and white wine. Simmer until vegetables are tender. Add potatoes and water to cover. Simmer until potatoes are tender. At this point, mash some of the potatoes to add body to the soup. Add milk, blending well. Add fresh rosemary at this point. Simmer awhile on low heat.

Yield: 4-6 servings

# ORIENTAL CHICKEN SOUP

*Clear liquid soups can be bland and uninteresting, or they can be succulent and mysterious. Recently a chicken soup I was making evolved into something else entirely when I added water chestnuts, Chinese vegetables, and a myriad of other interesting things. The addition of eggs gave it a nice finish, adding flavor and texture. After emptying everything in the pantry that even hinted of the Orient, including a couple of boxes of dried Ramen Noodle Soup, I became apprehensive. Had I overdone it? Was it going to be awful? Well, let me tell you, this soup was "to die for". I shared some with friends and they confirmed my opinion — the soup was indeed wonderful! My hubby said, "Marlyn, don't forget what you did to this soup." That stopped me dead in my tracks — what all had I dumped in that pot? My second try was perhaps not quite as great, but pretty close. I just thought of something — a can of Ro-tel tomatoes would give it zest... and how about some stuffed noodles... mushrooms... perhaps rice! I can't wait to make another batch of this wonderful stuff!*

1 (3-pound) fryer and
   6 boneless chicken breasts
2-3 quarts water
2 large onions, chopped
4 ribs celery, chopped
4 chicken bouillon cubes
Pepper and salt, to taste
Tony Chachere Seasoning, to taste

1 medium bell pepper, chopped
1 bag Oriental frozen vegetables,
   with noodles (your choice)
1 pkg. dried Oriental soup
   mix, with noodles
1 can sliced water chestnuts
½ cup green onion tops, sliced
2 eggs, well beaten

Place chicken and water in large stockpot and bring to a boil. When scum forms on top, remove it. When scum is removed, add next six ingredients. Bring to a simmer, cover and let cook about one hour, until chicken is tender, but not falling off the bone. Remove chicken and let cool. Meanwhile, add remaining ingredients, whisking in beaten egg last. Add more water if needed. At this point, add more seasoning or bouillon, if desired. Debone chicken and cut into pieces; add to soup. Freezes beautifully!

Yield: 12-14 servings

# SHRIMP AND CORN CHOWDER

*If you're in the market for a low fat chowder, this is your dish. It is excellent for both the waistline and the tastebuds. The unique blending of cilantro and poblano pepper make this soup a sure winner.*

1 poblano pepper
1 large sweet red pepper
Vegetable cooking spray
2/3 cup onion, chopped
2 teaspoons minced garlic
2 (10 ounce) pkgs. frozen whole
    kernel corn, thawed
2 cups 2% low fat milk, divided

2/3 cup evaporated skim milk
1½ teaspoons cornstarch
4 tablespoons water
½ teaspoon salt
1 pound medium shrimp,
    peeled and deveined
2 tablespoons minced fresh
    cilantro

Cut poblano pepper in half lengthwise. Remove seeds and membrane. Place pepper, skin side up, on a baking sheet; flatten with palm of hand. Broil 6 inches from heat, with electric oven door partially opened, for 15 minutes or until skin is charred. Place peppers immediately in ice water and chill for 5 minutes. Remove from water; peel and discard skins. Mince pepper and set aside. Coat a nonstick skillet with cooking spray and place on medium-high heat until hot. Add onion and garlic and saute until tender. Place onion and garlic mixture in bowl of food processor; add corn and process until smooth. Transfer pureed mixture to a large saucepan and stir in 1 cup of the milk. Cook over medium heat, stirring constantly for 15 minutes. Add remaining 1 cup milk. Cover and simmer on low heat for 10 minutes, stirring occasionally. Pour corn mixture into a strainer, and press with back of spoon to squeeze out liquid. Discard pulp remaining in strainer. Return corn mixture to saucepan and stir in evaporated milk. Combine cornstarch and water and add to corn mixture; stir well. Add diced pepper and salt. Bring to a boil, reduce heat and simmer uncovered for 20 minutes or until thickened, stirring often. Add peeled shrimp to chowder and cook over medium heat for about 5 minutes or until shrimp turns pink. Stir in minced cilantro. Serve piping hot, garnished with fresh cilantro sprigs.

Yield: 4-6 servings

Jillian (Jill) Leigh
Duplichan

# Salads

Salads come in many colors, sizes, shapes, flavors, and forms — tossed, fruit, pasta, marinated, layered, congealed. The entree you serve often determines the type of salad that will accompany the meal. It's simple to throw in a green salad with almost any menu. It was "required eating" in my home, therefore, I immediately acquired a dislike for it. I learned to flatten my lettuce and place it under my plate where Mom would discover it later when she cleared the table. By that time I was usually a block down the street on my getaway bike!

Salad dressings come in hundreds of varieties — Caesar, Italian, French, Russian, bleu cheese, poppy seed... After trying many bottled varieties of dressings, and tossing most in the garbage, I decided to stick with homemade. I try to keep at least three varieties on hand at all times. The featured dressings in this cookbook are our favorites.

Pasta salads have become extremely popular in the last few years. They are attractive, delicious, and nutritious. A big plus with pasta salads versus tossed green salads is that pasta salads can be made ahead and kept in the refrigerator, whereas green salads must be tossed and served immediately. Pasta salads also make delicious entrees, with chicken breast, shrimp or crabmeat tossed in.

As for fruit salads, tell the kiddies that it's dessert and "not good for them" and you've got yourself a winner! The kid who turns up his/her nose at eating fruit will beg for seconds if it's mixed with Cool Whip and miniature marshmallows!

## SIMPLE SALAD

*Why buy salad dressing when you can combine these simple basic ingredients for a delicious dressing on hand at all times.*

½ cup olive oil
3 tablespoons wine vinegar
1 teaspoon sugar
1 teaspoon garlic puree
Coarse ground black pepper
   and salt, to taste

1 teaspoon dry mustard
1 head Romaine lettuce
5 fresh mushrooms, sliced
2 hard-boiled eggs, sliced
Seasoned croutons
¼ cup Parmesan cheese

Place olive oil, wine vinegar, sugar, garlic puree, black pepper and salt in a pint jar; cover and shake well to blend. Refrigerate. Wash Romaine, spin dry and gently tear in large pieces. Toss salad dressing with Romaine, mushrooms, eggs, croutons and sprinkle with Parmesan. Serve immediately.

Yield: 4 servings

## ORANGE AND ONION SALAD

*This salad is refreshing, colorful and delicious with oriental cuisine — or any cuisine!*

2 tablespoons red wine vinegar
1 teaspoon Dijon mustard
½ teaspoon salt
Pinch cayenne pepper
Pinch coarsely ground black pepper
1 tablespoon honey

6 tablespoons vegetable oil
1½ teaspoons poppy seeds
½ small red onion, thinly sliced
1 (11 ounce) can mandarin
   oranges, drained
1 small head iceberg lettuce
½ cup sliced almonds, roasted

Combine first eight ingredients and blend well; chill. Place torn iceberg lettuce, well-drained mandarin oranges, onion slices, and almonds in a salad bowl. Toss with dressing and serve immediately.

Yield: 4-6 servings

## BLEU CHEESE ITALIAN DRESSING

*This popular dressing is featured in many cookbooks, in one form or another; it bears repeating...and trying. The olive oil/bleu cheese combination is scrumptious!*

1½ tablespoons garlic puree
1 teaspoon salt
½ teaspoon coarse grind pepper
¼ teaspoon celery salt
½ teaspoon cayenne pepper

½ teaspoon dry mustard
¼ cup red wine vinegar
½ cup extra virgin olive oil
½ cup Crisco oil
1 (4 ounce) pkg. bleu cheese, crumbled

Blend all ingredients, except olive oil, Crisco oil, and bleu cheese. Mash one-half of the bleu cheese and add to blended mixture. Add oils slowly and, using wire whisk, beat constantly until well blended. Stir in remaining crumbled bleu cheese. Let set out about 30 minutes before tossing with salad greens of your choice.

Yield: 1⅓ cups dressing

## CAESAR SALAD DRESSING

*This is a delicious Caesar dressing. One caution, the health authorities advise us to cook eggs well these days, so you may want to leave out the raw egg.*

½ cup Crisco oil
1 tablespoon garlic puree
1½ teaspoons salt
1½ teaspoons dry mustard
1 teaspoon coarse black pepper

3 tablespoons cider vinegar
2 teaspoons Worcestershire
1 teaspoon sugar
1 finely chopped anchovy
1 egg, well beaten (optional)

Combine all ingredients, except egg. Whisk together until well blended; add egg at this time. Toss with Romaine lettuce, croutons, mushrooms, and Parmesan cheese. Lay an anchovy on top of each individual salad. Serve with crisp toastpoints.

Yield: ½ pint

# SUSAN'S CITRUS SALAD

*My stepdaughter Susan lives in Seattle, where fresh produce and seafood abound! Susan describes this salad as a "light, colorful and refreshing salad to serve with a heavy meal or for a luncheon with a casserole and bread." Thanks go to Susan for this great salad.*

| | |
|---|---|
| 1 head butter leaf lettuce | ¾ cup raspberry vinegar |
| 1 pound Ruby Red grapefruit | ¼ cup olive oil |
| 1 pound naval oranges | ¼ cup orange juice |
| ½ small red onion | ⅛ teaspoon white pepper |

Wash, trim and tear lettuce into large pieces. Peel, section and remove seeds from grapefruit and oranges. Section and seed fruit over a small bowl and add any retained juice to the dressing. Slice onion in thin rings. Combine lettuce, fruit and onion rings in a salad bowl. For Dressing: Combine vinegar, olive oil, orange juice and white pepper in a jar and shake well to blend. Toss ⅓ cup of the dressing with salad just before serving.

Yield: 4-6 servings

# MEXICAN SALAD

*This Mex salad is light and adaptable to almost any menu, be it Mexican or American. If I am serving it with a meat entree, I often leave out the ground chuck. Delicious!*

| | |
|---|---|
| 1¼ pounds ground chuck | 1 small head lettuce, shredded |
| 1 can spicy chili beans, drained well | 2 small tomatoes, seeded & chopped |
| ⅓ pound shredded sharp cheddar | 1 medium bag Taco or plain |
| 1 large avocado, cup up | tortillas, coarsely crushed |
| 1 small red onion, sliced thin | ¼ cup Creamy Italian dressing |

Season meat with salt, red pepper and chili powder. Brown well and drain. Be sure that meat and chili beans are drained very well. Before serving, toss all ingredients and add dressing. Serve on large flat crisp tortilla or large lettuce leaf.

Yield: 6-8 servings

# CRAB/PASTA SALAD

*This salad was a favorite of mine many years ago at a popular local Italian restaurant, now closed. After many months of traveling across town for this delicious treat, I had eaten it enough to have a broad idea of how to make it. I finally felt secure enough to serve it to guests — they loved it! It is a beautiful, unique, and delicious Italian salad and is abundant enough to serve as a main meal.*

½ pound thin spaghetti
 or angel hair pasta
1 cup cracked Greek olives
½ bunch parsley, chopped
½ bunch green onion tops,
 chopped

1 bunch leafy lettuce leaves,
 cleaned
1 pound fresh lump crabmeat
1 medium tomato, quartered
 (for each individual serving)

Boil spaghetti; toss with Greek olives, ⅓ dressing, parsley, and green onions. Place lettuce leaves on six individual salad plates and top with spaghetti. Place crabmeat on top of spaghetti and garnish with tomato wedges on the side. Drizzle remaining dressing overall and serve with crusty French or Italian bread.

Dressing Ingredients:
1 cup olive oil
6 tablespoons wine vinegar
¼ cup lemon juice,
 freshly squeezed
3 tablespoons garlic puree
Dash of seasoned salt

Italian seasoning, to taste
Oregano, to taste
Coarsely ground black pepper
½ bunch parsley, chopped
½ bunch green onion tops,
 chopped

Combine all dressing ingredients, blending well. Dressing can be made a day ahead and refrigerated until ready to toss.

Yield: 6 servings

# PERFECT PASTA PLATTER

*If you're hosting a luncheon and looking for the perfect make-ahead salad, this is your baby. The tray can be prepared before guests arrive, leaving you free to enjoy your company. The pasta, garnished and framed with colorful vegetables, makes for a real eye catcher! Use your imagination by adding anything your heart desires — grated Feta or Parmesan cheese sprinkled on the pasta, a mild Edam, Swiss or Gouda cheese, cut in chunks, shrimp in place of the turkey and ham — after all it's your party! This eye-catching salad will be a hit with your guests; I guarantee it!*

12 ounces vermicelli
Leafy red lettuce
Leafy green lettuce
1 jar marinated mushrooms
1 jar marinated artichoke hearts
1 small purple onion, sliced thin

3 baby yellow squash, sliced thin
10-12 whole cherry tomatoes
½ pound smoked turkey,
   cut in chunks
½ pound honey ham, cut in chunks
Parsley sprigs for garnish

Dressing:
1/3 cup wine vinegar
2 teaspoons Dijon mustard
2 teaspoons minced garlic
½ teaspoon salt
½ teaspoon sugar

½ teaspoon fresh ground pepper
3 tablespoons olive oil
3 tablespoons vegetable oil
Juice of ½ lemon

Combine vinegar and next five ingredients. Gradually add olive oil, vegetable oil and lemon juice; whisk mixture until well blended. Boil vermicelli until al dente with about one tablespoon salt; drain. Mix vermicelli with dressing, tossing well. Add turkey and ham chunks mixing well; chill at least one hour. Line a large platter with red and green leafy lettuce and spoon pasta into the center; sprinkle with parsley. Arrange mushrooms, artichoke hearts, onion, squash, and cherry tomatoes around pasta. Garnish top of pasta with parsley sprigs, colorful bell pepper rings or cherry tomatoes. Serve with crispy toastpoints or crackers of your choice.

Yield: 6 servings

# CHINESE CHICKEN SALAD

*My daughter Debbie shared this salad recipe with me when we spent Christmas in Oklahoma with her and her family. It is delightful — and great for the waistline.*

3-4 cooked chicken breasts, shredded
1 (10 oz.) bag finely shredded cabbage
5-8 green onions, chopped
4 tablespoons sesame seeds
½ cup sliced almonds
3 pkgs. Ramen noodles

Dressing:
¾ cup oil
6 tablespoons red wine vinegar
4 tablespoons sugar
Seasoning packets from
    Ramen noodles

Mix all dressing ingredients the day before serving for flavors to blend. Toast sesame seeds and almonds in 350 degree oven for 10 minutes. Prepare Ramen noodles, without seasonings. To serve, toss together all ingredients and blend in dressing.

Yield: 6 servings

# TOMATO/PASTA SALAD

*This is a pasta salad that is a true "keeper"; it will keep in the refrigerator for a week to ten days, however, it doesn't last that long in our home.*

1 pound curly vermicelli, crumbled
1 large red onion, chopped
1 bell pepper, chopped
3 fresh tomatoes, chopped and deseeded
2 small cans sliced black olives

Dressing Ingredients:
1 large bottle Italian dressing
1 pkg. Good Seasons
    Italian Dressing (Dry)
½ bottle Salad Supreme
    by McCormick

Boil vermicelli until al dente; drain well. Toss with onions, bell pepper, tomatoes, and ripe olives. Blend in dressing.

Yield: 6-8

# SHRIMP/CRAB SALAD

*This salad is one of my oldest recipes and, although I have tried others through the years, it remains my favorite. When my children were small, this fit the bill for boating trips on hot summer days. Everyone loved it except Danny, the gourmet, who brought along his can of Vienna Sausages! This makes a great stuffing for avocados or tomatoes.*

3-4 pounds spicy boiled
   shrimp, coarsely chopped
3 hard-boiled eggs, chopped
4 tablespoons sweet pickle
   relish, drained well
2 stalks celery, chopped
1 small jar chopped pimento

4 stalks green onion tops, chopped
$^2/_3$ to ¾ cups Hellmann's
   mayonnaise
Cayenne pepper, to taste
Salt and black pepper, to taste
1 pound white or backfin
   crabmeat, picked and drained

Toss together all ingredients except crabmeat and mix well. Carefully fold in crabmeat. At this point, add a little more mayonnaise if it seems dry. Toss LIGHTLY and refrigerate. Delicious served on saltine crackers.

Yield: 6 servings

# EASIEST SLAW IN TOWN

1 bag shredded slaw mix
¾ cup Hellmann's mayonnaise
¼ cup bottled Ranch dressing
3 hard-boiled eggs, chopped

Salt and pepper, to taste
Garlic powder, to taste
3 stalks green onion tops,
   chopped

Combine slaw mix with hard-boiled eggs and green onion tops. Mix mayonnaise and Ranch dressing and toss with slaw mix. Add salt, pepper and garlic powder to taste.

Yield: 6 servings

Variation: Substitute your favorite Italian dressing for the Ranch for a change in flavor.

# BROCCOLI SALAD

*I'm not a fan of raw broccoli, but this salad is really great.*

1 large or 2 small bunches
   fresh broccoli
1 pound lean bacon, fried crisp
½ cup golden raisins
½ cup walnuts, coarsely chopped
½ cup green onions, chopped

Dressing:
1 cup Hellmann's mayonnaise
½ cup sugar
1 tablespoon apple cider vinegar

Mix Dressing ingredients and refrigerate overnight. Clean and cut fresh broccoli. Crumble bacon. Toss together all dry ingredients. Add dressing and toss together until well blended. Refrigerate.

Yield: 8 servings


# BLACK EYE PEA SALAD

*This salad is a marvelous accompaniment for almost any meat, especially smoked meats or fried chicken. It's truly southern, ya'll!*

4 cups cooked, drained
   black eye peas
1 cup Crisco oil
¼ cup red wine vinegar
1 tablespoon pureed garlic
1 stalk celery, chopped
1 teaspoon sugar

²/₃ cup red onion, sliced thin
1 red bell pepper, sliced thin
1 deseeded jalapeno pepper,
   chopped fine
1 small can sliced black olives,
   drained

Combine all ingredients except peas. Add mixture to peas and toss well. Marinate 2 days in refrigerator. Delicious served with tortilla chips.

Yield: 8 servings

# GRANDMA JUMEL'S POTATO SALAD

*This potato salad has been handed down for generations by my mother's family. Seems like she brought this salad to hundreds of covered dish dinners. That dear lady put so much love into making this salad! To me, it is the best potato salad in the world and although time consuming to prepare, it is well worth the effort. In my catering days, it took lots of nerve on my part to go through this lengthy process when feeding 100 plus people, but the customers loved it, so I made it!*

8 medium red potatoes
4 hard-boiled eggs
2 tablespoons cider vinegar
1 heaping tablespoon mustard
2 cups Hellman's mayonnaise
5-6 green onion tops, chopped
3 large stalks celery, chopped

½ bell pepper, chopped
²/₃ cup olives with pimentos,
  chopped
1 small jar diced pimentos,
  drained
Salt and black pepper, to taste
½ teaspoon garlic powder

Boil red potatoes in their skins; when cool, peel and chop.

For Dressing: With fork, mash egg <u>yolks</u> and slowly blend in cider vinegar until all lumps are out. Whip in prepared mustard. Add Hellman's mayonnaise, a little at a time until well blended and smooth. Mix potatoes with chopped green onions, celery, olives, pimentos, and bell pepper. Lightly fold in mayonnaise mixture. Add chopped egg whites, salt, pepper and garlic powder until seasoned to your taste. Chill and serve.

Yield: 10-12 servings

Variation: Boil potatoes and eggs in water seasoned with Crab Boil. When tender, remove from seasoned water and dump into water one pound peeled shrimp. Boil shrimp about 10 minutes, drain and chop coarsely. Add to above potato salad recipe. Sprinkle salad with Parmesan cheese for added flavor. (Note: this was definitely not a part of my ancestor's recipe — I'm sure my grandmother is turning over in her grave!)

*This is the Potato Salad that originated the saying:*
*"So Good...Make You Slap Your Mama!"*

# "TO DIE FOR" PASTA SALAD

12 ounce curly vermicelli, broken into pieces

Dressing Ingredients:
½ cup Crisco oil
¼ cup fresh lemon juice
2 tablespoons Tex-Joy Steak
    Seasoning
3 drops Tabasco sauce

Salad Ingredients:
1 (#2) can chopped black olives,
    drained
1 large jar chopped pimento,
    drained
6-8 green onion tops, chopped
½ cup Hellmann's mayonnaise
1 pound boiled shrimp or
    crawfish (optional)

Boil vermicelli until tender, about 5 minutes — do not overcook. Drain well. While vermicelli is HOT, add the dressing ingredients and mix well. When mixed, add the remaining salad ingredients. Toss in either shrimp or crawfish. Chill and serve.

Yield: 8 servings

# ITALIAN PASTA SALAD

2 pkgs. stuffed tortellini
    (in deli section)
½ pound fresh mushrooms, sliced
1 jar marinated artichoke hearts
1 can hearts of palm, sliced
1 can gourmet baby corn
2 stalks celery, sliced coarsely

1 small red onion, sliced thin
1 can cracked Greek olives
1 pound spicy boiled shrimp, whole
1 bottle Greek or Caesar Dressing
1½ cups grated mozzarella cheese
Garlic powder and cayenne,
    to taste

Drain vegetables. Toss all ingredients; place in sealed container in refrigerator. Served chilled on lettuce leaf.

Yield: 12 servings

# APPLE SALAD

*My mother-in-law, Louise Monette discovered this topping/dressing recipe in a magazine many years ago. The dressing is also great as a topping for fresh fruit.*

8-10 Red Delicious apples,
   peeled and cut in cubes
2 medium cans pineapple chunks,
   well drained
²/₃ cup raisins
1 cup pecans, coarsely chopped

3 stalks celery, chopped
2 cups miniature marshmallows
2 cups Cool Whip
2 cups Hellmann's mayonnaise
2 tablespoons fresh lemon juice
1 teaspoon nutmeg

Toss together apples, pineapple, raisins, pecans and celery. Mix dressing ingredients and fold lightly into fruit mixture. When ready to serve, fold in marshmallows.

Yield: 8-10 servings

# PEAR SALAD

1 large head red or green curly
   lettuce, washed
4 fresh pears, peeled and sliced
¹/₃ pound bleu cheese, crumbled
½ cup walnuts, coarsely chopped
½ cup sugar

Dressing Ingredients:
²/₃ cup olive oil
¹/₃ cup red wine vinegar
2 teaspoons Dijon mustard
Salt and pepper, to taste
2 tablespoons sugar

Mix dressing ingredients and chill, preferably overnight. To poach pears: simmer in ½ cup sugar and enough water to cover pears, until tender; drain. Cut pears in half, removing seed. To toast walnuts: place on cookie sheet and bake in 300 degree oven for about 15 minutes, stirring once. To serve, arrange lettuce on individual plates. Top with 2 pear halves and sprinkle with bleu cheese and walnuts. Drizzle with dressing before serving.

Yield: 4 servings

## LEMON CREAM CHEESE SALAD

*This is our favorite congealed salad. It is light and tasty — marvelous for holidays.*

1 large lemon gelatin
1 cup boiling water
8 ounces cream cheese
1 (3 ounce) jar pimento, drained

1 cup cold water
1 medium can crushed pineapple,
   with juice
1 (8 ounce) Cool Whip

Mix gelatin and boiling water. Place cream cheese and pimento in food processor and blend well. Add cream cheese mixture to boiling gelatin mixture. Blend together well with wire whisk. Remove from heat and add cold water and crushed pineapple with juice. Cool in refrigerator until consistency of firm jelly. Fold into Cool Whip. Place in mold and refrigerator. Serve on lettuce leaf.

Yield: 6 servings

## BLUEBERRY CONGEALED SALAD

*This versatile congealed salad blends in well with almost any main dish, whether it be fancy or plain. Thanks go to my dear friend Ann May for sharing a treasured favorite.*

1 small lemon gelatin
1¼ cups hot water
8 ounces cream cheese, softened

2 cups Dream Whip
2 small pkgs. strawberry gelatin
2 cans blueberries, reserve juice

Dissolve lemon gelatin in hot water; add softened cream cheese. Prepare Dream Whip by package directions, using one envelope which makes two cups; blend into cream cheese/gelatin mixture and chill until firm. Add enough water to blueberry juice to make 3 cups and heat to boiling. Dissolve strawberry gelatin into boiling blueberry juice and water. Chill until thickened, then fold in the blueberries. Pour blueberry mixture over lemon/cream cheese mixture and chill until ready to serve.

Yield: 12 servings

## STRAWBERRY DELIGHT

*This salad brings back fond memories of a dear friend, Ann Boullion or "Little Annie" who passed away in 1997. We loved to tease that Annie could not "boil water". She showed up with this dish one day and proved she could indeed "boil water".*

| | |
|---|---|
| 1 large strawberry-banana gelatin | 2 cups chopped pecans |
| 2 (10 ounce) frozen strawberries | Middle Layer: |
| 1 cup boiling water | 1 cup sour cream |
| 1 large can crushed pineapple, well drained | 1 (8 ounce) cream cheese, softened |

Dissolve gelatin in boiling water; add thawed strawberries, drained pineapple, and pecans. Pour one-half mixture into 13x9x2 inch baking dish and chill until set. For middle layer, beat softened cream cheese with sour cream. Spread over the first layer of set gelatin. Carefully add remaining gelatin/fruit mixture to form top layer. Chill until well set.

Yield: 10 servings

## COKE/CHERRY MOLD

| | |
|---|---|
| 1 small pkg. strawberry gelatin | 1 cup pitted dark sweet cherries |
| 1 small pkg. cherry gelatin | 1 (13 ounce) can pineapple tidbits |
| 1 (8 ounce) cream cheese | 7 ounces Coca Cola |
| ¼ cup Hellmann's mayonnaise | 1 cup chopped pecans |
| 1 cup boiling water | |

Blend cream cheese and mayonnaise until smooth. Dissolve gelatin in boiling water and stir in cheese mixture, blending well. Drain cherries and pineapple and add juice to gelatin mixture. Blend in Coca Cola. Chill until thick; remove from refrigerator and fold in cherries, pineapple and nuts. Pour into a greased mold and chill.

Yield: 8-10 servings

# HOLIDAY CRANBERRY SALAD

*I got my first taste of this wonderful congealed salad on Thanksgiving when my editor at <u>Portfolio Magazine</u>, Kay Chance was our guest for the holiday dinner. Kay, a fabulous cook, contributed this dish to our meal, along with delicious potato salad and deviled eggs. My granddaughter Jillian, a picky eater, scarfed down almost all of the marvelous deviled eggs. I think we'll have Kay share all our holidays, since her cooking skills are "right up there" with her writing skills! I thank her for sharing this great recipe.*

| | |
|---|---|
| 1 cup ground raw cranberries | 1 cup pineapple juice |
| 1 cup sugar | 1 large can crushed pineapple, |
| 1 small pkg. lemon gelatin | drained well |
| 1 small pkg. raspberry gelatin | 1 cup celery, finely chopped |
| 1 cup hot water | ¾ cup broken pecans |

Combine cranberries and sugar. Dissolve both gelatins in hot water; add pineapple juice and chill until mixture is just beginning to set. Add all other ingredients and chill.

Yield: 6-8 servings

# THE SIMPLEST SALAD OF THEM ALL

*This easy salad is perfect for the novice in the kitchen. It's so easy, I tend to forget it and go for the more complex salads these days. That's a mistake because this one is truly delicious. Many years ago for a dinner party I stuffed this mixture into cone-shaped paper cups and unmolded them and decorated them as Christmas trees — was I proud!*

| | |
|---|---|
| 1 (15 ounce) can fruit cocktail | ½ pint sour cream |
| 1 small pkg. mini marshmallows | ⅔ cup coarsely chopped pecans |

Drain the fruit cocktail well. Place in medium bowl and toss in the remaining ingredients. Chill until firm. Serve on lettuce leaf.

Yield: 4-6 servings

Courtney Claire Czarnecki

# Entrees

# Meats

Since my husband and I both love meat, there are few vegetarian meals in our home, but with all the recent warnings about the dangers of fat and cholesterol, I am very aware of the cuts of meat that I buy. We limit our beef intake to once a week and purchase only lean cuts, such as round steak, ground round or sirloin, with an occasional ribeye thrown in when we're living dangerously!

We eat lots of chicken. What is more economical? What is more compatible with any herb, spice or vegetable? Chicken fits into almost any diet, depending on how you cook it, and its versatility is unbelievable! We can turn it into pot pies, stews, baked, soups, spaghetti sauces, tacos, dressings — even fancy-sounding dishes like Kiev or Coq Au Vin! You name it — Chicken can become it!

In our home, we also enjoy lots of pork tenderloin and veal. We love sausage, but due to its high fat content, we limit our intake. There's an old saying, "don't ever ask how sausage or boudin are made." I'm sure that's true, unless you stick with the low-fat varieties. Our son, Danny, provides us with venison sausage from his deer hunting bounty every year, so we are able to enjoy this lean succulent sausage with jambalaya, red beans, or as a special Sunday morning breakfast.

Whether your entree consists of beef, chicken, pork or veal, what is important is that you gather around the table as a family as often as you can arrange it. The city, with all its problems and traumas may be just outside your door, but inside your home, all should be tranquil at the time of day when you and your family sit down to share a meal.

# CHICKEN AND DUMPLINGS

*As a picky teenager, I sampled my first chicken and dumplings in the home of a friend. I knew I was in trouble when I saw the huge tureen filled with enormous lumps of soggy dough and thick white globs of gravy. I remember this as one of the longest meals of my life — it was simply awful! Years later, as a young bride, I concocted what I call my South Louisiana version of this dish — thin light dumplings and a gravy that is truly "so good... make you slap your mama!" Browning the chicken makes for a richer gravy, both in color and flavor. This dish is delicious served with petit pois peas or baby limas, salad and hot rolls. Using a frying chicken is the quick version, but a hen, cooked for two hours will provide a much richer gravy.*

| | |
|---|---|
| 1 (3-4 pound) frying chicken, cut up | ¼ cup cooking oil |
| Salt, pepper, and garlic powder, to taste | 1-2 cups water |
| | 3 chicken bouillon cubes |

Season chicken pieces with salt, pepper and garlic powder. In heavy Dutch oven or black iron pot, brown chicken well in Crisco oil. When browned, add water to about 1 inch above the level of the chicken pieces. Bring to a boil and add bouillon cubes. Cover and simmer slowly for one hour or until chicken is tender. Remove chicken from pot; cool and debone. After deboning chicken, drop dumplings into simmering gravy, one at a time, being careful to keep them from touching as you drop them in. The gravy will be very thin, but thickens as the flour-coated dumplings are added, resulting in a thick, rich gravy. Simmer dumplings on low heat until they are tender. Return deboned chicken to gravy, being careful not to tear up dumplings.

Dumplings:

| | |
|---|---|
| 1 cup flour | 1 egg, beaten |
| 1 pinch salt | Cold water, scant |
| 1 piece shortening (size of an egg) | |

Mix dumpling ingredients together, adding a little water if dough seems dry. Flour work surface liberally, roll dough out thin and cut into narrow strips.

Yield: 4 servings

## GOURMET CHICKEN SUPREME

*This succulent dish is my version of a signature dish of a renowned French Quarter Restaurant.*

6 boneless, skinless fryer breasts
2 cups sour cream
2 tablespoons crushed garlic
4 teaspoons Worcestershire
2 teaspoons paprika
2 teaspoons coarse grind pepper

¼ cup fresh lemon juice
4 teaspoons celery salt
1¾ cups bread crumbs
½ cup butter
3 teaspoons salt
½ cup vegetable shortening

Wipe chicken well after cleaning. In large bowl, combine sour cream with next six ingredients. Dip chicken breasts in sour cream mixture, one at a time. Roll dipped chicken in bread crumbs and arrange in 13x9x2 inch baking dish. Melt butter and shortening together in a small saucepan and spoon half over chicken. Bake chicken in a 350 degree oven, uncovered. Remove and spoon remaining butter/shortening mixture over chicken; bake 15 minutes longer.

Yield: 6 servings


## HONEY MUSTARD CHICKEN

¼ cup Dijon-wine mustard
¼ cup honey
¼ teaspoon curry powder

2 tablespoons margarine, melted
4 boneless, skinless chicken
   breasts
¹/₃ cup bread crumbs

Mix together mustard, honey, curry and melted margarine. Dip chicken breast in mixture and sprinkle lightly with bread crumbs. Place in 13x9x2 inch baking dish that has been sprayed with cooking spray. Cover and bake in 350 degree oven for one hour.

Yield: 4 servings

# CHICKEN CACCIATORE

*This dish is so elegant and delicious, you will forget you're eating healthy!*

6 boneless chicken breasts
Salt, pepper, garlic powder
    lemon pepper, to taste
¼ -½ cup olive oil
2 (10 ounce) cans plum tomatoes,
    reserve juice

1 medium bell pepper, cut in strips
1 large onion, cut in chunks
½ pound fresh mushrooms
    or 1 large can whole mushrooms
½ cup dry white wine
Oregano, basil, parsley, to taste

Season chicken with garlic powder, lemon pepper and salt.  In a large skillet, brown chicken in olive oil; add drained tomatoes, bell pepper, onion and mushrooms  Pour juice from tomatoes and white wine over all and sprinkle lightly with oregano, basil and parsley. Cover skillet and slowly simmer for one hour.  Serve with spaghetti — or just an Italian salad and crusty bread.

Yield:  6 servings

# PEACHY CHICKEN

*This easy, delicious dish gets high marks for appearance and flavor. The mingling of peaches and bacon makes for a winning combination. Wonderful served with wild rice.*

6 boneless chicken breasts
2 strips lean bacon
Onion powder, to taste

Celery salt, to taste
1 large can peach halves, packed
    in juice, not syrup

Fry bacon in large skillet; cool and crumble.  Season chicken with celery salt and onion powder; brown in bacon drippings.  Add peaches and juice. Cover skillet and simmer for about 45 minutes.  Transfer chicken and peaches to a serving platter and sprinkle crumbled bacon over peach halves.

Yield:  6 servings

## LADYE'S CHICKEN APRICOT

*My sister-in-law, Ladye White shared this recipe with me. It is both nutritious and easy to prepare. Preparation time of 15 minutes certainly lends itself to our busy schedules.*

6 chicken breasts or thighs
1 bottle Russian Dressing
1 small jar apricot preserves
1 pkg. dry onion soup mix

½ cup water
Salt, coarse grind black pepper,
    and garlic powder, to taste

Place chicken pieces in 13x9x2 inch baking dish. Mix together the remaining ingredients and drizzle over chicken pieces. Bake uncovered in 350 degree oven for 1 hour.

Yield: 4-6 servings

## ROSEMARY CHICKEN ALA DENIS

*A few years ago I featured a delightful man named Denis Ricou, in my food column. Not only did he share super game recipes, but he returned the day after the interview bearing gifts — fresh herbs from his garden, relishes, and seasonings. One of the benefits of writing about people is the new friends you make — people like Denis Ricou. I thank him for introducing me to the "wonders" of rosemary; I've never been the same since!*

1 (3 pound) frying chicken
2 tablespoons fresh rosemary,
    chopped or 1 tablespoon dried
Juice of ½ lemon

1 stick butter
    (do not substitute with margarine)
Salt and pepper, to taste

Mix rosemary, lemon juice and softened butter; put one-half of the mixture under the skin of clean chicken. Salt and pepper chicken lightly. Put remaining rosemary, lemon and butter mixture in carcass of chicken. Place in roaster and bake uncovered in 325 degree oven for 1½ hours.

Yield: 4-6 servings

# THE ORIGINAL CHICKEN AND RICE CASSEROLE

*This casserole is the first one I ever learned to prepare as a young bride. It became my "company dish" when a rare guest told me it was delicious. Being somewhat less than versatile in those early days, I always served it with baby limas, salad and fluffy rolls. There are many casseroles in my repertoire now, but this old favorite is still on the "much loved" list in my family. As an added bonus, it's low in both calories and fat grams.*

| | |
|---|---|
| 1 frying chicken, cut up | 3-4 stalks celery, chopped |
| Salt and pepper, to taste | ½ cup chopped parsley |
| ¼ cup cooking oil | 1 cup raw, long grain rice |
| 1 bunch green onions, chopped | 1 (14 ounce) can chicken broth |

Season chicken pieces with salt and pepper. Heat cooking oil in large skillet and brown chicken pieces. While chicken is browning, coat a 2-quart casserole with cooking spray. Place rice in the bottom of casserole dish and sprinkle with one-half of the vegetables. When chicken pieces are browned, place on top of rice and vegetables. Pour chicken broth on top of chicken pieces and top with remainder of vegetables. Cover and bake in a 350 degree oven for one hour.

Yield: 4 servings

*When frying chicken, cut it up and soak the pieces in buttermilk for several hours before battering for a wonderful flavor!*

# CHICKEN AND ASPARAGUS CASSEROLE

*This splendid casserole was served at a bridal luncheon that I attended several years ago. The hostess, Mona Morgan, was gracious enough to share her recipe. I recently featured it in my column where it drew raves. Rich in flavor and texture, this succulent casserole will delight even the most discriminating guest.*

6-8 large boneless chicken breasts
1 medium onion, chopped
1 stick margarine
½ pound fresh mushrooms, sliced
   and sauteed in margarine
1 can cream of mushroom soup
1 can cream of chicken soup
1 (5⅓ ounce) can evaporated milk

½ pound sharp cheese, grated
½ teaspoon Tabasco
2 teaspoons soy sauce
½ teaspoon salt and pepper
1 teaspoon Accent
2 tablespoons pimiento, chopped
3 cans cut asparagus, drained
⅔ cup slivered almonds

Boil chicken breasts in well-seasoned water until tender; cool, take out and tear into bite-sized pieces. Set aside. In Dutch oven, saute onion in margarine and add remaining ingredients, except asparagus and almonds. Simmer sauce until the cheese melts, stirring to keep it from sticking to the bottom of the pot. To assemble, place a layer of one-half the chicken in a 15x10x3 inch baking dish, a layer of one-half the asparagus tips and a layer of one-half the sauce. Repeat layers, ending with the sauce. Top with almonds. Bake uncovered in a 350 degree oven until hot and bubbly, about 30 minutes — do not add any liquid even if it appears to be dry!

Yield:  12 servings

*When buying chicken, find a local market
that sells fresh fryers.  There is no
comparison in flavor, especially
if you're serving it fried!*

# MARLYN'S CHICKEN TETRAZZINI

*This dish was our most requested item at Occasions Catering. It's a recipe I created for a covered dish dinner years ago. Thank goodness I had the good sense to write it down because Chicken Tetrazzini became my signature dish when I began my business. I made it so often, my husband soon began to complain, "if my supper tonight is leftover Chicken Tetrazzini from a luncheon, don't bring it home — I'll eat a grill cheese sandwich". And, this was from a man who never complains, but will eat anything I put on the table! I hope you enjoy this delicious dish as much as we have. Make plenty — it freezes well.*

Boiling Ingredients:
1 (3½ pound) fryer or
   6-8 large chicken breasts
1 large onion, chopped
4 ribs celery, chopped

Tony Chachere's seasoning
4 bouillon cubes
Cayenne pepper and salt, to taste

1½ sticks margarine
1 large onion, chopped
1 medium green bell pepper,
   chopped
½ pound mushrooms, sliced
½ cup flour
3 cups homogenized milk

1½ pounds Velveeta, cut in chunks
1 bunch green onion tops, chopped
1 pound vermacelli or thin
   spaghetti, broken in thirds
White pepper, to taste
Parmesan, to taste

Boil chicken in water seasoned with onion, celery, bouillon cubes and seasonings until tender, about one hour. Remove chicken from broth, RESERVING BROTH. Cool chicken and debone; cut into chunks. Set aside. While chicken is boiling, saute onion and bell pepper in margarine until tender. Add mushrooms and saute about 10 minutes. Blend in flour, stirring constantly. Slowly, stir in milk, blending well. Add Velveeta and stir on low heat until completely melted. Add green onion tops and white pepper. Boil spaghetti in the broth that you boiled chicken — JUST UNTIL DONE. Drain spaghetti and toss with sauce. Fold in chicken pieces. Place in sprayed baking dish and sprinkle with Parmesan. Bake uncovered in 350 degree oven for about 30 minutes. Do not overbake.

Yield: 10 servings

# GAME

*Though I realize a number of you are avid hunters and do prepare a lot of game, there are many folks who do not have access to this succulent fare; therefore, I feature only a few of my favorites. In South Louisiana we cooked and served wild game like others serve chicken. Let's face it — if the freezer was full, we cooked it! I was thankful that no one ever went squirrel hunting — or nutria hunting!! If you haven't cooked game, give it a try — there are marvelous things you can do with it! I remember the first time I cooked a venison rump roast, my children never had a clue it was not beef and went back for seconds. My little urchins had the belief that it's not pork and cabbage one ate on New Years Day, but venison or duck!*

## VENISON TIPS

1 venison rump roast or
   backstrap, cut in chunks
½ cup dry sherry
½ cup cooking oil
4 tablespoons flour
1 medium onion, chopped
2 stalks celery, chopped

1 small bell pepper, chopped
1 cup water
½ cup dry sherry
2 tablespoons Worcestershire
½ pound mushrooms, sliced
2 chicken bouillon cubes
Rice or noodles

Marinate venison in dry sherry for at least two hours. In black iron pot or heavy Dutch oven, brown meat on high heat. Add onions, celery, bell pepper, and mushroom slices. Sprinkle flour over meat and vegetables and blend well. Slowly add water, Worcestershire and dry sherry; bring to a boil, throw in chicken bouillon cubes and simmer for an hour or two on low heat. Serve with rice or noodles.

Yield: 6-8 servings

# VENISON RUMP ROAST

The simplest way: Cut slits in a 4-6 pound venison rump roast and stuff it with garlic. Salt and pepper roast well; roll in lightly salted flour. In large Dutch oven, brown roast quickly in a mixture of ¼ cup cooking oil and ¼ stick margarine. When roast is brown, add 3 tablespoons Worcestershire, 1 cup cream sherry, and one can mushrooms with juice. Cover and pop in 325 degree oven; bake for about 2 hours. Be careful not to overcook as venison is lean. Serve with rice or mashed potatoes. Delicious!

Serves: 4-6

# HEAVENLY PHEASANT

*Our son-in-law Randy brought home an abundance of pheasant last winter, so our daughter Debbie learned to cook it in a variety of ways. She shared some of this delicious meat with us, along with some of her recipes. This one is our favorite.*

| | |
|---|---|
| 2 pheasants, cut in quarters | 2 stalks celery, chopped |
| Salt and cayenne pepper, to taste | 1 cup chicken broth |
| 2 tablespoons rosemary | 1 cup cream sherry, divided |
| 8 slices lean bacon | 1 cup heavy cream |
| 1 medium onion, sliced | Cooked rice |

Rub pheasant quarters with salt and cayenne pepper. Sprinkle the pieces with rosemary. Wrap one slice bacon around each piece of pheasant. Place in roaster. Sprinkle ¼ cup of sherry over the birds and bake in 450 degree oven for 20 minutes, uncovered. Remove from oven and add onions, celery, and chicken broth. Cover roasting pan; reduce heat to 375 degrees and roast pheasant for 45 minutes or until tender. Remove pheasants from roaster and keep warm. Put roaster on top of stove and add the remainder of the sherry and the heavy cream. Bring to a boil and reduce the heat to simmer, stirring constantly. When the gravy has thickened, drizzle some over pheasant and serve the rest with rice.

Yield: 4-6 servings

# HELEN'S POT ROAST DUCK

*I have been cooking ducks in various ways for many years, but this one "takes the prize". We had this on New Years Day at the home of friends, Helen and Harold Turner. After tasting the multi-talented Helen's pot roast duck, I threw my recipe away! Don't let the length intimidate you — it requires little "handling" time, but actually cooks itself.*

Day Before:
3-4 ducks, teals, mallards,
   or pintails, cleaned and skinned
Salt, pepper, cayenne pepper and
   cumin, to taste

½ cup cooking oil
3 large onions, chopped

Season whole ducks with salt, pepper, cayenne pepper and cumin; brown in large Dutch oven in oil. Add onion and simmer about 30 minutes. Cool and refrigerate.

Day of Serving - first step:
1 can chicken broth
2 cans Ro-tel tomatoes

3 tablespoons garlic puree
2 medium bell peppers, chopped

Place reserved duck, vegetables and drippings back in Dutch oven. Add chicken broth, Ro-tel tomatoes, garlic, celery, and bell pepper. Place in 300 degree oven, cover and simmer for 4-5 hours. In other words, forget it! After 4 or 5 hours, remove ducks from pot, cool and debone, leaving meat in big pieces.

Second Step:
½ cup cooking oil
½ cup flour
2 large onions, chopped
3 stalks celery, chopped

1 medium bell pepper, chopped
2 tablespoons garlic puree
1 quart water
Creole seasoning, to taste

In a heavy pot, make a dark roux, stirring constantly. Add celery, onions, bell pepper, seasoning and simmer on low fire until tender. To roux, add gravy from roasting ducks and deboned duck meat. Cover and simmer low for about one hour. AT LAST — SERVE AND ENJOY!

Yield: 10-12 servings

# RUMP ROAST FAMILY STYLE

*My mother cooked rump roast this way, and her mother before her. My children loved it and my husband loves it also. I've never tasted any better, or simpler. The au jus gravy this roast makes "all by itself" is delicious on rice or mashed potatoes — or simply on bread! If you desire the gravy thickened a little, instructions follow.*

| | |
|---|---|
| 1 (4-5 pound) lean beef rump roast | ¼ cup cooking oil |
| Salt and pepper, to taste | ¼ cup margarine |
| ½ cup chopped garlic, or | 3 tablespoons Worcestershire |
|    whole garlic pods | ½ cup cream sherry |
| ½ cup flour | Cooked rice or mashed potatoes |

Season roast with salt and pepper; cut deep slits in two or three areas of roast and stuff with garlic. Lightly flour roast, and brown well in mixture of oil and margarine in Dutch oven (or black iron pot). When brown, add Worcestershire and sherry. Cover roast tightly and bake in 325 degree oven for about 30 minutes a pound. Test roast for tenderness before removing from oven; when roast is tender, remove from Dutch oven and place on serving platter. Place pot on stove top and thicken gravy as follows: Mix two tablespoons cornstarch with about two-thirds cup cool tap water; stir until smooth. Bring drippings from roast to a simmer and slowly add mixture, stirring until thickened. At this point, if you desire more gravy, add a little water and one teaspoon chicken bouillon for more richness.
Yield: 6-8 servings

*Once long ago while dining in a restaurant with my "overactive" three kids, an elderly gent passed our table. With a look of amusement, he leaned down and whispered in my ear, "Madam, dining out with youngsters is akin to taking a hamburger to a banquet, is it not?" Amen!*

# ED'S SWISS STEAK

*I take no credit for this one — it belongs to my husband, Ed who has a distinct flair for cooking beef, or any other meat for that matter. Your family will love it.*

2 pounds beef round steak
Garlic puree, to taste
½ cup flour
Salt and pepper, to taste

¼ cup bacon drippings
1 large onion, chopped
1 (14 ounce) can whole tomatoes

Trim edges of steak and rub with garlic puree. Using a mallet, pound flour, salt and pepper into steak to flatten and tenderize. Heat bacon drippings in large skillet; add onion and simmer. Remove onions and sear steak in the drippings. Return onions to skillet and add tomatoes. Cover and bake in 325 degree oven for 1½ hours. Serve with mashed potatoes.

Yield: 4 servings

# SIMPLE BEEF CASSEROLE

2 pounds lean stew meat
  or sirloin beef tips
Salt, lemon pepper, garlic
  powder, to taste
2 large onions, sliced in rings

1 can cream of mushroom soup
½ cup dry sherry
½ pound sliced fresh mushrooms,
  sauteed in butter
Parsley, to taste

Season meat with salt, lemon pepper and garlic powder; brown well in black iron pot or Dutch oven. When meat is browned, add onion rings and saute about 5 minutes. Mix soup with sherry and pour over meat and onions. If more gravy is desired, add about one-half cup water also. Add sauteed mushrooms. Add parsley, sprinkling lightly. Cover pot and bake in 275 degree oven for 2-3 hours. Serve with rice or noodles.

Yield: 4-6 servings

# BRISKET, OVEN STYLE

*This is a great family dish or company dish! Simply pop it into the oven and forget it.*

1 (6 pound) lean brisket
  (do not remove fat layer)
1¼ cups ketchup
¾ cup water
2 teaspoons vinegar
2 tablespoons Worcestershire

1 tablespoon brown sugar
1 teaspoon salt
1 teaspoon paprika
1 teaspoon chili powder
1 teaspoon cayenne pepper
1 teaspoon Liquid Smoke

Lay brisket, fat side up in a heavy roasting pan. Mix remaining ingredients well and heat. Pour over brisket. DO NOT COVER roasting pan. Bake in 300 degree oven for one hour. Remove roasting pan from oven and cover lightly with foil; reduce oven temperature to 275 degrees and return to oven. Bake covered for 4-5 hours, basting with sauce about every 30-40 minutes. Slice thin and serve.

Yield: 8-10 serving

# DEB'S FAST AND EASY MEATLOAF

2-3 pounds ground beef
2 eggs
Salt, pepper, garlic puree, to taste
²/₃ cup bread crumbs
1 frozen hamburger bun

2 tablespoons Italian Seasoning
4 slices mozzarella cheese,
  divided
2-3 slices ham
1 small can tomato sauce

Mix together first six ingredients, blending well. Form 2 large patties. On top of one, layer mozzarella and ham. Place remaining patty on top and press edges together well to seal. Pour tomato sauce on top. Bake 1 hour and 15 minutes in 325 degree oven. Remove from oven and top with 2 slices mozzarella; return to oven until cheese is melted.

Yield: 6 servings

# ME ME'S FRENCH SPAGHETTI AND DAUBE

*This is a South Louisiana version of one of the most popular dishes in the world — spaghetti. The recipe originated in the 1800's in the home of my mother's grandparents. Many decades later, my Mom was in demand to prepare this delicious dish for my brother's and my friends. Once they tasted it, they were hooked, and their Moms simply could not make it. It is made with a rich roux, giving it a dark red color, and is unlike any spaghetti gravy I have ever tasted. If you're wondering what a "daube" is, in South Louisiana it is the name for a very thick cut of round steak or roast. This very lean cut of beef has virtually no fat and must be cooked long and slow.*

3-4 pound round roast
Salt, pepper, garlic puree to taste
4-5 fresh garlic pods, peeled
²/₃ cup cooking oil, divided
½ cup flour
2 large onions, chopped
1 small bell pepper, chopped
3 tablespoons pureed garlic

1 small can tomato paste
2 small cans tomato sauce
2 cups water, or more
1 tablespoon sugar
2 bay leaves
Parsley, to taste
4-5 stalks green onions, chopped
1½ pounds spaghetti

Season roast with salt, pepper and garlic puree; make deep slits in two or three places in roast and stuff with garlic pods (or chopped garlic). In black iron pot or large Dutch oven, brown roast in one-third cup oil. Remove browned roast and add remaining oil. Blend in flour and, stirring constantly, make a dark brown roux. Add onions, bell pepper, garlic and simmer about 15 minutes, stirring. Stir in tomato paste and blend well. Add tomato sauce and simmer about 10 minutes longer. Slowly stir in water and blend well; add sugar and bay leaves. Adjust seasonings to suit your taste. Return roast to pot, cover and simmer on low heat for two or three hours, stirring occasionally, until roast is tender. Add green onions and parsley about 30 minutes before it's done. Slice roast and serve with spaghetti and gravy.

Yield: 8-10 servings

Variation: Substitute a large fresh pork roast for the "daube" for another wonderful and different taste treat.

# DAWN'S LASAGNA

*Attempting to copy a recipe of Dawn Barnett's is like following the famous chef Graham Kerr around! Dawn took a version of Lasagna from an old Junior League cookbook and simply "took off with it!" Every year she made it for my birthday dinner and invited all our friends — what a hit that dinner was! This is about as close as I could get to what she does, considering she does something a little different every time. Thanks Dawny Bird!!!!*

2 pounds ground beef
1 clove garlic, minced
2 tablespoons parsley flakes
1 tablespoon basil
1½ teaspoons salt
2 cups whole tomatoes
2 (6 ounce) cans tomato paste
1½ pounds Italian sausage
1 (8 ounce) package sliced
   pepperoni

2 (16 ounce) cartons cream
   style cottage cheese
3 beaten eggs
2 teaspoons salt
1 teaspoon black pepper
3 tablespoons parsley flakes
⅔ cup Parmesan cheese
1½ pounds mozzarella cheese

Brown ground beef and add next six ingredients. Prepare Italian sausage by simmering in a skillet until grease has cooked out; when done, drain, slit skin and remove meat. Crumble meat well. Add sausage and thinly sliced pepperoni to beef mixture. Simmer uncovered until thick, about 45 minutes, stirring often. While gravy is simmering, cook noodles until tender; drain and rinse in cold water. Combine cottage cheese with next five ingredients; set aside. To layer: place one-half of noodles in bottom of greased 13x9x2 inch baking dish (or deeper lasagna dish). Spread one-half of cottage cheese mixture over noodles; add one-half of mozzarella cheese and one-half meat mixture. Repeat layers. Sprinkle some Parmesan over top. Bake in 375 degree oven for 30-40 minutes. Let sit 15 minutes before cutting into squares. Freezes well.

Yield: 8 servings

*No matter the recipe, my own personal taste dictates that I add a little sugar to ALL tomato-based sauces to cut the acid taste.*

# VEAL PARMIGIANA

*Veal is young beef — usually no more than eight weeks old. It is delicate in taste and it is expensive. I enjoy preparing veal scallops, or "scallopini", which are thin slices of veal. Veal cutlets, chops, or rump roast are equally delicious. Whatever cut you choose, veal is a versatile dish which can be prepared many ways. Veal Parmigiana is an Italian dish which is best with veal cutlets. This easy, make ahead dish is an elegant delicacy to serve guests — it tells them "you are special".*

| | |
|---|---|
| 6 veal cutlets | 3 small cans tomato sauce |
| Salt and pepper, to taste | 1 teaspoon sugar |
| 1½ cups dry bread crumbs | 1½ teaspoons ground basil |
| ⅓ cup Parmesan | 1 teaspoon oregano |
| 2 eggs, slightly beaten | ½ teaspoon thyme |
| 1 cup chopped onion | 1 teaspoon dried Italian seasoning |
| 2 tablespoons chopped garlic slices | 1 (8 ounce) pkg. Mozzarella |
| 6 tablespoons olive oil, divided | ½ cup grated Romano or |
| 1 (16 ounce) can whole tomatoes | Parmesan cheese |

Mix bread crumbs and 1/3 cup Parmesan. Salt and pepper cutlets on both sides, then dip each in eggs, then in crumbs. Heat 4 tablespoons olive oil in skillet; add veal and saute. When lightly browned on both sides, remove and set aside. In skillet, saute onions and garlic in two tablespoons olive oil until soft. Add next seven ingredients. Cover and simmer for 20 minutes. To bake, spoon a little sauce into a large, shallow baking dish. Place one layer of cutlets in dish and cover each cutlet with a slice of mozzarella. Spoon remaining sauce over veal. Sprinkle with Parmesan. Bake uncovered in preheated 350 degree oven for 45 minutes, until hot and bubbly. Serve with spaghetti. Freezes well.

Yield: 6 servings

Variation: If you have a favorite bottled spaghetti sauce that you think is wonderful, there's no law that says you have to make your own sauce. It is not a sin to make a meal simple, as long as it's good! Simply place your veal and mozzarella in the baking dish, drizzle the sauce over it and sprinkle with Parmesan. So easy!

# VEAL SCALLOPINI

*There are many variations of Veal Scallopini, all of them delicious. This is one of our favorite company dishes, served either Italian style, with fettuccini, Italian salad, and garlic bread, or served a little more formal, with fluffy Lemon Rice, Brandied Glazed Baby Carrots, Caesar Salad, and homemade rolls. It is so marvelous, it would be memorable simply served on toast rounds! Veal Scallopini must be cooked and served immediately, so it's best for a dinner party to prepare everything but the veal before the guests arrive, unless you are serving fettucine, which also must be assembled and served immediately. As your guests are finishing up their salad course, quickly saute the veal, deglaze it in the wine sauce and place it directly on each individual plate before it is "whisked" to the dining room. This assembly line method of preparing the plates can be tricky at times when there are 40-50 guests waiting for the entree and can "age" one considerably; therefore, I prefer to prepare this dish for small gatherings only.*

8 paper thin scallops of veal
½ cup flour
1 teaspoon salt
½ teaspoon pepper

4 tablespoons olive oil
½ cup dry white wine
Juice of 1 freshly squeezed
    small lemon

Combine flour, salt and pepper. Lightly coat each veal slice with flour mixture. Heat olive oil in large skillet to medium-high heat. Add veal and cook two minutes on each side. Remove veal from skillet and set aside. Turn heat up and pour wine and lemon juice into skillet drippings. Let cook down for about one minute and return veal to skillet; coat or deglaze each side with sauce and serve immediately.

Yield: 4 servings

Tip: If you're watching your fat and calories, this dish is for you! Served with Lemon Rice and Brandied Carrots, it's truly a heart healthy meal.

# SHERRIED VEAL

*This is my husband Ed's dish. It is what I like to call a "comfort" food — delicate and tender, yet served with a somewhat hearty gravy. Marvelous with mashed potatoes!*

4 veal cutlets
½ stick butter
Salt and pepper, to taste
¼ cup flour
1 can sliced mushrooms, in butter

½ stick butter
3 chopped green onion stalks
½ cup dry sherry
1 (14 ounce) can prepared
  brown gravy

Salt and pepper veal cutlets and flour lightly. Saute in ½ stick butter until brown. Place in 13x9x2 inch baking dish. For sherry sauce: saute onions and mushrooms in butter. Add sherry and brown gravy. Bring to a low simmer and cook slowly about 5 minutes, stirring often. Pour sauce over cutlets in baking dish. Cover with foil, place in 350 degree oven and bake for one hour. This dish can be prepared a day ahead.

Yield: 4 servings

# VEAL CHOPS ALA NANCE

*This dish comes from the kitchen of my talented friend and former partner, Susan Nance. Susan not only cooks wonderful stuff, but she makes it look beautiful as well. This classic dish will delight guests.*

4 thick cut veal chops
Paul Prudhommes Pork and
  Veal Seasoning, to taste

Tex Joy Seasoning, to taste
2-3 tablespoons extra
  virgin olive oil

Rub chops liberally with Pork and Veal Seasoning and Tex Joy Seasoning. Drizzle lightly with olive oil and gently rub in. Place over medium-hot coals and cook until tender, about 20-30 minutes, depending on thickness of chops. Or, place on rack in oven and broil on each side about 5-7 minutes.

Yield: 4 servings

## PORK CHOPS MONETTE

*This is a simple family dish, but the flavor is indescribable! It is easy and takes no time to put together and place in the oven. Any cut of pork will do — plain ole pork chops or thick boneless pork chops are wonderful! Try it on your family.*

6 thick cut pork chops
   boneless or with bone
Salt and pepper, to taste
¼ cup flour

4-5 tablespoons cooking oil
2 cans cream of mushroom soup
½ cup dry white wine

Salt and pepper pork chops and dust lightly with flour. Heat cooking oil in large skillet and quickly brown pork chops on both sides. Place single layer in long baking dish. Mix cream of mushroom soup and white wine and pour over chops. Cover with foil and bake in 350 degree oven for one hour. Serve with fluffy rice, black eyed peas and cornbread!!!

Yield: 4-6 servings

Tip: If you have a large Magnalite skillet with cover, you can brown chops, pour soup and wine on top, cover and bake. This will give you one less item to wash!

## SKILLET PORK CHOPS

6 thick pork chops
Salt and pepper, to taste
3 tablespoons cooking oil

1 onion, sliced into 6 rings
6 lemon slices
½ cup light vermouth

Season chops and brown on one side in a heavy skillet; turn browned side over and put an onion slice and a lemon slice on each chop. Pour vermouth over chops, cover skillet and steam chops about 40 minutes, or until tender. Great with potatoes au gratin and a green vegetable.

Yield: 4-6 servings

# SCOTTY & LADYE'S PORK TENDERLOIN

*During my brother Scotty's years of overseas travel with the U.S. Special Forces, he and his wife, Ladye enjoyed sampling cuisine from all over the world. This recipe is one they acquired while on a NATO assignment in Naples, Italy. This succulent meat is beyond description! It is exotic as a dinner entree, sliced thin for luncheon sandwiches, or adorning a beautiful cocktail party tray. It was #1 among my customers at Occasions.*

2 pounds pork tenderloin
½ cup chicken broth
½ cup soy sauce
¼ cup cream or dry sherry

3 tablespoons sugar
1 teaspoon pureed garlic
1 teaspoon red food coloring

Cut each tenderloin across the grain (at an angle) into two or there equal pieces. Mix broth, soy sauce, sherry, sugar, garlic, and red food coloring. Stir until sugar dissolves. Add meat, cover and marinate 24 hours, turning occasionally. Remove from marinade and place on grill 4-6 inches above *low* fire. Cover grill and cook 25 minutes. Turn and baste with marinade often while grilling. Do not overcook.

Yield:  4 servings

# GRILLED HONEY CHOPS

¼ cup dry white wine
2 tablespoons lemon juice
¹/₃ cup honey
2 tablespoons soy sauce
1 tablespoon pureed garlic

1 teaspoon minced ginger
¼ cup finely chopped green
   onion tops
Salt and pepper, to taste
6 thick boneless pork chops

Combine all ingredients except pork chops. Marinate pork chops in this mixture overnight. Remove chops from marinade and grill over medium heat with grill lid closed 10-12 minutes on each side. Do not overcook.

Yield:  4-6 servings

## SUSAN'S MAPLE/PECAN PORK CHOPS

*The combination of Dijon mustard, ground ginger and maple syrup give spark to this pork dish — add the crunch of pecans and you've got a winner! My partner, Susan Nance takes the bows for this one. Try this at your next dinner party — you'll knock'em dead!*

4 boneless lean pork chops
2 teaspoons Dijon mustard
3 tablespoons flour
½ teaspoon ground ginger
3 teaspoons cooking oil

2 tablespoons maple syrup
  (or lo-fat variety)
2 tablespoons chopped
  roasted pecans

Place chops between 2 sheets of heavy-duty plastic wrap and flatten to one-fourth inch thickness, using a meat mallet. Spread Dijon mustard on both sides of chops. Combine flour and ginger and dredge pork chops. Coat a large skillet with cooking spray; add oil. Heat to medium/hot, add chops and cook three minutes on each side, or until browned. Combine maple syrup and pecans and add to pork chops, stirring to coat well. Cover skillet and simmer about 25-30 minutes longer, until tender. Sprinkle celery leaves for garnish.

Yield: 4 servings

## FAMILY PORK AND RICE

6 lean pork chops
1 cup raw rice
1 fresh tomato, sliced
1 bell pepper, sliced

1 onion, sliced
1 can beef bouillon
½ cup water
Salt and pepper, to taste

Coat 13x9x2 inch baking dish with cooking spray. Place raw rice in bottom of casserole. Salt and pepper pork chops and brown in skillet. Place chops on top of rice. Place 1 slice tomato, onion, and pepper ring on top of each chop. Pour bouillon and water over all. Cover tightly with foil and bake in 375 degree oven for 1 hour. Very good... and easy!

Yield: 4-6 servings

## COMPANY PORK LOIN

*This elaborate dish will draw raves at your next dinner party. Paired with a light rice dish or your favorite stuffing you have a sure winner. This is also delicious sliced and served chilled with tea rolls as an appetizer.*

1 (4-6 pound) boneless pork loin
2/3 cup dry sherry
2/3 cup soy sauce
1 tablespoon ground ginger
Thyme and dry mustard, to taste

2 tablespoons garlic puree
1 cup apple jelly
1 tablespoon soy sauce
2 tablespoons dry sherry

Combine one-half cup sherry, soy sauce, ginger and garlic; pour over roast. Marinate eight hours, turning once or twice. Remove meat and reserve marinade. Bake uncovered for 20 minutes per pound in 325 degree oven, basting often with marinade. Melt apple jelly in microwave oven and add soy sauce and 2 tablespoons sherry; cool. Place pork loin on a rack in a roaster and spoon glaze over. Repeat glazing method until a glaze has built up on roast. Slice and serve.

Yield: 6-8 servings

## QUICK AND EASY HAM STEAK

*Ham steaks are available in the meat counter at your supermarket and are normally securely packaged in a sealed plastic wrapping, ready to pop in your freezer for future meals. As an added bonus, they thaw quickly. Open a can of candied yams for a side dish. Top that off with black eyed peas or green beans and a pot of cornbread! Delish!*

1 thick cut ham steak
2 tablespoons prepared mustard

2 tablespoons brown sugar

Mix together mustard and brown sugar. Rub top of ham steak with this mixture. Place ham steak on foil-lined baking sheet and slit a couple of corners with a knife so ham won't curl up when it begins cooking. Place in preheated oven and bake about 20 minutes, uncovered.

Yield: 4 servings

# LOUISE'S BAKED HAM

*There is a wide choice when it comes to choosing ham — Virginia, honey cured, mesquite smoked, hickory smoked, boiled — it can be baffling to the shopper. There's the old fashioned picnic ham, with bone in, which usually requires more baking. There's the gourmet boneless ham, some of which have all the flavor of "cured" cardboard! There are various methods of preparing the "fully-cooked" ham after you purchase it. We have all eaten ham, often the Virginia ham, which was so salty, we were as bloated as a beached whale for days! We are advised to boil this ham to cut the salt. Then, there's the "sweet" ham — so studded with pineapple, cherries and cloves, it's nauseous. For my mother-in-law, Louise Monette, "ham" signified "heaven" — the lady loved it! After years of experimenting with different ham baking methods, she found this marvelous preparation and shared it with me. I beg you to try it! You will never bake it any other way again!*

| | |
|---|---|
| 1 lean, boneless ham | 1 tablespoon cider vinegar |
|   or ham of your choice | 1 teaspoon dry mustard |
| 8-10 whole cloves | 3 tablespoons concentrated |
| ¾ cup brown sugar |   frozen orange juice, thawed |
| 1 tablespoon flour | |

Stud ham in several places with cloves. Place ham in roaster and bake, uncovered in 350 degree oven for about 45 minutes. While ham is baking, combine remaining ingredients, blending well. Remove ham from oven, spoon mixture over ham and return to oven; bake an additional 30 minutes. Slice and serve.

Yield: 6-8 servings

Tip: Cut leftover ham into chunks. Prepare macaroni and cheese, your favorite way. Toss in ham and serve with petit pois peas, salad, and fluffy rolls.

# SAUSAGE JAMBALAYA

*Now we're talking South Louisiana! Whether you make this dish with sausage only, or opt to add chicken or shrimp, it's delicious! If I'm in a pinch for ideas for a quick dinner, I pull out a package of my son Danny's spicy venison and pork sausage, especially made for him from his deer hunting bounty. As it's tossed in the old black iron pot, one thing is for certain — there'll be good eating tonight!!*

2 pounds smoked sausage,
  cut in 1 inch pieces
1 large onion, chopped
1 medium bell pepper, chopped
1 stalk celery, chopped
3 tablespoons pureed garlic
1 can whole tomatoes
1 can Ro-tel tomatoes (optional)

1 teaspoon sugar
Thyme, bay leaf, to taste
Cajun seasoning, Tabasco, to taste
1 tablespoon chicken bouillon
4 stalks green onion, chopped
Parsley, to taste
3-4 cups *cooked* rice

Saute sausage pieces in black iron pot or Dutch oven. Add onion, bell pepper, celery, and garlic; simmer about 10 minutes or until vegetables are tender. Drain tomatoes, reserving liquid; add to vegetables, and "fry down" a little. Add juice from tomatoes and blend well. Add remaining ingredients, except green onion, parsley and rice. Simmer for about 1 hour on low heat. Add green onion, parsley and fold in cooked rice, blending until well mixed. Serve with salad, crusty French bread or cornbread.

Yield: 8-10 servings

Tip: If adding deboned chicken or shrimp, do not add until the last 20-30 minutes of cooking. Adding shrimp is a special treat — there's something about the body and richness it lends to the tomato gravy that is memorable.

*There are many delicious Cajun jambalaya mixes
on the grocery shelves. Have no guilt about using them,
if you and your family are pleased. The bottom line: If it's
delicious, who cares where it originated?*

# RED BEANS AND SAUSAGE

1 pound bag dried red kidney beans
2 pounds smoked sausage,
  cut in 1" pieces
2 medium onions, chopped
1 bell pepper, chopped
½ pound cooked ham pieces,
  (optional)

4 tablespoons chopped garlic
Cajun seasoning, to taste
3 tablespoons chicken bouillon
  or 5 chicken bouillon cubes
1 tablespoon sugar
1-2 cups water, approximate
1 cup green onion tops, chopped

Soak beans in water overnight. Rinse and drain; set aside. Saute sliced sausage in black iron pot or Dutch oven until browned. Remove from pot. In sausage drippings, saute onions, bell pepper and garlic. Add water, beans, ham and all remaining ingredients, except green onion. At this time, adjust water; it should cover beans. Cover pot and simmer on low fire for 2-3 hours or until beans are tender, stirring occasionally. Add green onions. Serve with fluffy rice.

Yield: 8-10 servings

# SAUSAGE/RICE CASSEROLE

1 pound bulk sausage,
  hot or regular
1 large onion, chopped
2 stalks celery, chopped
½ bell pepper, chopped

1 can chicken broth
½ cup water
1 cup fresh mushrooms, sliced
¼ cup parsley, chopped
1 cup raw rice

Brown sausage, remove from skillet. Leaving about 3-4 tablespoons sausage drippings in skillet, saute onion, celery and bell pepper; add mushrooms and saute 5 minutes. Combine sausage, chicken broth, water, parsley, and rice. Pour mixture into a 2-quart casserole, cover tightly and bake in 350 degree oven for 1 hour. Toss lightly before serving.

Yield: 4 servings

## LEG OF LAMB IN THE GREEK STYLE

*My husband introduced me to lamb, and a Greek friend gave me tips on cooking it. One evening I served Greek style lamb to guests. The gentleman was retired Air Force and his only comment was, "we had lots of <u>mutton</u> in the Service". I had a reformed "mutton" eater when that dinner ended! He not only cleaned his plate, but he went back for more! With the lamb that evening I served Lemon Rice, Asparagus Casserole, and Greek Salad.*

| | |
|---|---|
| 1 large leg of lamb | Salt and pepper, to taste |
| 4-5 garlic pods, peeled | Dried oregano leaves, to taste |
| Lemon juice, to taste | ¼ cup olive oil |

With a sharp knife, make 2-3 deep gashes in lamb. Stuff with garlic pods. Salt and pepper lamb; rub with lemon juice, sprinkle with oregano leaves and pat down. Carefully drizzle lamb with olive oil. Bake uncovered in 325 degree oven until tender, about 20-30 minutes per pound.

Yield: 4-6 servings

## LEFTOVER LAMB CURRY

| | |
|---|---|
| ½ stick margarine, divided | ½ cup raisins |
| 1 teaspoon curry powder | 1 large onion, sliced |
| 2-3 cups diced leftover lamb | 2 stalks celery, chopped |
| 2 teaspoons flour | 2 apples, cored, pared, sliced |
| 1 cup chicken broth | 1 tablespoon lemon juice |

Melt 2 tablespoons margarine in a saucepan. Blend in curry powder; set aside. Melt remaining margarine in a skillet and brown the lamb pieces. When brown, sprinkle flour over lamb and stir in reserved margarine and curry mixture. Blend well. Slowly add chicken broth, stirring well. When sauce is bubbling, add raisins, onion, celery, and apple. Stir in lemon juice and cook slowly for about 20 minutes. Serve with rice.

Yield: 4-6 servings

# Entrees
# Seafood

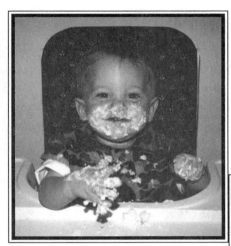

*Alec Scott Daniel*

Seafood! We Southerners have fashioned our cuisine around the seafood industry, especially shellfish — shrimp, oysters and crabs. When it comes to versatility, it would take an entire chapter of this book to list the hundreds of ways it can be prepared.

We who are fortunate to live in the south are blessed with an abundant supply of seafood, and if you can believe the "fish" stories, you'll believe that there is nowhere else on earth where one can find any bigger or tastier shrimp, crabs or oysters. I certainly believe it! A person who hails from Maine will quickly tell you about the gigantic lobsters to be enjoyed in that neck of the woods. My stepdaughter, Susan, who lives in Seattle, will show you the gigantic Dungeness crab or the most succulent salmon for which that area is known. Seafood is marvelous, no matter where it originates.

My children grew up on the water in South Louisiana where we enjoyed shrimping each and every year when the shrimp season opened. Nothing can describe the beauty and wonder of sitting in a boat, watching the sunrise over the lake. Sunrise signifies it's time to drop the net and begin dragging. The only greater thrill than the breathtaking sunrise is watching as the net is pulled up, filled with shrimp, crabs and a myriad of other creatures. It was a unique experience for children, as well as parents!

The seafood recipes in this chapter are all very special to me. They represent many years of sharing memorable meals with memorable friends.

# FRIED CATFISH

1 cup milk
¼ cup prepared mustard
Salt and cayenne pepper, to taste
1 tablespoon onion powder
1 egg, beaten
2 tablespoons garlic puree
1 teaspoon Greek seasoning
½ cup beer

2 cups cooking oil
8-10 catfish filets
²/₃ cup cornmeal
¹/₃ cup flour
1 tablespoon Greek seasoning
Salt and cayenne pepper, to taste
Garlic powder, to taste
Juice of one lemon

Mix well the first eight ingredients; add fish filets and marinate at least 4 hours. Drain filets in a colander. Mix cornmeal, flour, Greek seasoning, salt, pepper and garlic powder. Dip fish filets in cornmeal mixture and fry in medium oil. Drain and drizzle with lemon juice.

Yield: 4 servings


# HUSHPUPPIES — BEST OF THE BEST!

*There are frozen hushpuppies available in the supermarket, but there is no substitute for the homemade ones. My buddy from Lake Charles, Jerry Arbaugh, who to my knowledge, has never used a recipe in his life, taught me to make these many years ago. They are truly the best! Since I have no chapter on "Breads", I felt the appropriate place for this recipe was with Fried Fish — hope you enjoy!*

1 cup cornmeal
1 cup self-rising flour
1 teaspoon sugar
1 teaspoon baking powder
1 egg

1 onion, grated
Cayenne and garlic, to taste
¾ cup milk (approximate)
²/₃ cup green onion tops, chopped
1-2 cups Crisco oil

Mix all ingredients, except oil. Drop by tablespoons into medium-hot oil. Be sure oil is not too hot or they will brown too fast and not cook thoroughly on the inside.

Yield: 2-3 dozen

# SEAFOOD FEAST

*Try this delicious, rich casserole for your next dinner party. Teamed up with a light rice dish, Caesar Salad, crusty French bread and white wine, it is an elegant feast which will impress even the most discriminating guest. On the day before your party, prepare the casserole and refrigerate it. Clean Romaine lettuce for the salad and spin almost dry — place loosely in a plastic bag and refrigerate. Prepare the salad dressing, grate Parmesan cheese, and boil two or three eggs for slicing. Prepare the French bread with butter, garlic and light parsley and wrap it in foil, ready for baking. Voila!! That leaves you free on the day of your dinner party to pamper yourself so you will be glamorous for your guests.*

1 stick butter
1 (8 oz.) pkg. cream cheese
3 Tablespoons butter
1 large onion, chopped
1 small bell pepper, chopped
3 ribs celery, chopped
½ lb. fresh mushrooms, sliced
1½ lbs. shrimp, peeled & deveined

1 can Cream of Mushroom soup
1 Tablespoon pureed or
   finely-chopped garlic
Tabasco, to taste
1 teaspoon white pepper
1 cup cooked rice
1 lb. fresh white or lump crabmeat
8 ozs. sharp Cheddar cheese, grated
Cracker crumbs

Melt butter in 2 quart saucepan; add cream cheese and stir until cheese is melted. In heavy Dutch oven, sauté onion, bell pepper and celery in 3 Tablespoons butter. Add sliced mushrooms and shrimp and simmer about 5 minutes, stirring constantly. Add the melted cream cheese and butter mixture. Blend in soup, seasonings and rice. Carefully fold in crabmeat. Place in a greased 13x9x2 inch casserole. Toss Cheddar cheese and cracker crumbs together and sprinkle over top. Bake in 350 degrees for approximately 30 minutes, until bubbly and golden brown.

Yield: 8 servings

*In planning your dinner party menu,
include as many make-ahead dishes as possible.
Whatever you do, don't experiment with new recipes.
Stick with tried and true!*

# SEAFOOD IMPERIAL

*This is another delightful party casserole which can be made ahead. So easy!*

1 large bell pepper, diced
1 small jar chopped pimentos
Salt and white pepper, to taste
1 tablespoon dry mustard
3 tablespoons Hellmann's
  mayonnaise

2 eggs, lightly beaten
3 tablespoons dry sherry
1 pound lump crabmeat
1 pound medium boiled shrimp
Paprika, to taste

Mix diced pepper and pimentos. Add salt, pepper, dry mustard, mayonnaise, eggs and sherry. Mix well. Add shrimp and carefully fold in the crabmeat. Place in a greased casserole dish. Sprinkle lightly with paprika and bake in 350 degree oven for 15-20 minutes until hot and bubbly.

Yield: 6 servings

# ED'S SALMON CROQUETTES

*Everyone loves salmon croquettes! When dining out, I often find the croquettes too "bready", with very little salmon. These easy-to-make croquettes are absolutely divine. They are delicious paired with macaroni and cheese and petit pois peas or baby limas.*

1 large can red sockeye salmon
1 medium onion, chopped fine
2 eggs, beaten

1 tube buttery crackers, crushed
Salt, black pepper and Cayenne,
1 cup cooking oil

Drain salmon and pick it clean of all grissle and bone. Mix with remaining ingredients except cooking oil, reserving some cracker crumbs for coating croquettes. Form croquettes into patties and roll in reserved crackers. Heat oil in skillet to medium heat and fry croquettes until done throughout. Drain well.

Yield: 6 croquettes

# CLAM SPAGHETTI

*This is my most requested recipe. We first sampled this treat while visiting my stepdaughter Susan and her family in Seattle. It rated right up there with her marvelous Dungeness crabs. It is hard to describe this dish — unique, pure, tantalizing, bold — but let it suffice to say that it is not your run-of-the-mill, heavy Italian fare. Don't let the length of the recipe intimidate you — it's very simple to prepare. Be sure to have all the ingredients on hand, as you add them step-by-step. It is important not to alter this recipe — it is perfect as it is.*

½ cup + 1 tablespoon olive oil
1 teaspoon dried cayenne peppers
1 large onion, chopped
3 large garlic cloves, chopped
　or 2 tablespoons garlic puree
1 tablespoon dried basil
1 tablespoon oregano leaves
Salt and pepper, to taste

3 cans chopped or minced clams,
　drained, reserve liquid
1 pound spaghetti or vermicelli
1 cup fresh parsley, chopped
Grated Parmesan or Romano,
　to taste
1 small jar chopped pimentos,
　drained

1. Put olive oil in Dutch oven; heat slowly. Add dried red peppers, chopped onion, and garlic. Cook slowly for 30 minutes or until onions are soft.
2. Add the basil, oregano, salt and pepper and reserved liquid from clams. Continue to simmer until some of the liquid is reduced down. Keep warm.
3. Bring large pot of water to a boil. Add a tablespoon salt and a tablespoon of oil. Cook spaghetti until just al dente (about 5-6 minutes).
4. As pasta is cooking, add clams, parsley and 3 tablespoons cheese to the sauce. Simmer at low heat for five minutes; add pimento.
5. Drain pasta; stir into sauce and toss. Sprinkle generously with grated Parmesan and serve directly from the pot.

Yield: 4-6 servings

Tip: After step 2, you can keep sauce warm while you entertain guests; complete final steps and toss with spaghetti when ready to serve.

# SHRIMP SPAGHETTI

*While the Clam Spaghetti is enhanced by serving it with light wine, this robust Italian dish blossoms when served with hearty burgundy wine.*

²/₃ cup oil
2 onions, minced
3 cloves garlic, minced
¾ cup celery, chopped
¾ cup bell pepper, chopped
1 small can tomato paste
1 small can tomato sauce
1 teaspoon sugar

1 can mushrooms, sliced
1 cup red wine
2 pounds peeled shrimp
Parsley, finely chopped
Green onion tops, chopped
½ teaspoon sweet basil
1 pound spaghetti

In heavy pot, saute onions, garlic, celery and bell pepper in oil until onions are clear and tender. Add tomato paste, tomato sauce, sugar, mushrooms and red wine. Simmer slowly until oil rises to the top. Add shrimp, parsley, basil and green onions. Continue cooking over low heat about 20 minutes. Serve over hot spaghetti.

Yield: 4-6 servings

# SHRIMP VERMICELLI

*This recipe is a favorite of my son's wife, Carol. Busy with four young children, Carol finds this dish easy to prepare and perfect for entertaining.*

1 stick butter
½ cup green onions, chopped
½ pound fresh mushrooms
2 cloves garlic, minced

1½ pounds peeled shrimp
8 ounces vermicelli
1 cup grated Parmesan

Saute green onions and mushrooms in butter; add shrimp and garlic. Boil vermicelli until al dente, about 5 minutes, drain and toss with sauce. Add Parmesan and serve.

Yield: 4 servings

## FRENCH SHRIMP IN SHELLS

*Another of my husband's signature dishes, French Shrimp in Shells is a gourmet dish, whether served as a first course or as an entree. It features a delicate, superb sauce which will tempt you to "sop" your bread in it until the plate is clean.*

| | |
|---|---|
| 4 tablespoons butter | Pepper and paprika, to taste |
| 4 tablespoons flour | ¼ cup dry sherry |
| ½ teaspoon salt | 1½ pounds boiled shrimp |
| 1¼ cups milk | ²/₃ cup grated Parmesan |

Melt butter and stir in flour. Add milk slowly and stir until thickened. Stir in spices, shrimp, and sherry. Pour into baking shells or ramekins and sprinkle with Parmesan. Broil until cheese turns a golden/brown color. Serve immediately.

Yield: 4 servings

## SHRIMP WITH WILD RICE

| | |
|---|---|
| ½ cup flour | 1 cup fresh mushrooms, sliced |
| 1 cup melted margarine, divided | 2 pounds boiled shrimp |
| 4 cups chicken broth | 2 tablespoons Worcestershire |
| ½ teaspoon white pepper | Few drops Tabasco |
| 1 cup onion, thinly sliced | 1 small box Uncle Bens Wild & |
| ½ cup bell pepper, thinly sliced | Long Grain Rice |

For white sauce, add flour slowly to one-half cup melted margarine and cook until smooth. Gradually add chicken broth. Cook on low heat until thickened. Add white pepper and set aside. Saute onion, bell pepper and mushrooms in remaining one-half cup margarine; remove vegetables with a slotted spoon, leaving margarine drippings in skillet. Combine white sauce, vegetables and remaining ingredients. Place in two greased, shallow two-quart casserole dishes. Bake at 325 degrees for about 45 minutes until hot and bubbly.

Yield: 8 servings

## QUICK AND EASY ETOUFFEE

1 stick margarine
1 large onion, chopped
1 tablespoon garlic puree
2 stalks celery, chopped
½ pound fresh mushrooms, sliced
2 pounds peeled shrimp

1 tablespoon Worcestershire
½ cup green onion, chopped
¼ cup parsley, chopped
¼ cup cornstarch
½ cup cool, tap water
½-⅔ cup dry vermouth or wine

Saute onions, celery and garlic in margarine in large skillet until tender. Add mushrooms and simmer about five minutes longer. Add shrimp and wine and simmer about 15 minutes. Add Worcestershire, parsley and green onions. Mix cornstarch in cool water until smooth and stir enough into simmering gravy until thickened. Serve with fluffy rice.

Yield: 4-6 servings

## DEB'S SHRIMP CREOLE

*This recipe for Shrimp Creole is my daughter Debbie's, and our favorite.*

4 tablespoons flour
5 tablespoons Crisco oil
1 large onion, chopped
1 tablespoon chopped garlic
½ cup celery, chopped
¼ cup bell pepper, chopped
6-8 green onions, chopped

1 can (8 ounce) tomato sauce
1 can water
Salt and pepper, to taste
2 tablespoons Worcestershire
1 teaspoon Tabasco
2 pounds raw, medium shrimp,
    peeled and deveined

Add flour to oil in heavy Dutch oven and cook on medium heat, making a rich dark roux, stirring constantly to prevent scorching. Add remaining ingredients except shrimp and season to taste. Cover, turn heat to low and simmer slowly for 30-40 minutes. Add shrimp and cook slowly for another 20 minutes. Serve with fluffy, steamed rice.

Yield: 6 servings

## MARY'S SHRIMP CASSEROLE

*At a recent dinner party in her home, my friend Mary Rademacher served this marvelous dish. It is undoubtedly one of the best seafood dishes I've ever tasted. Each and every guest went back for seconds! Thanks Mary!*

12 large mushrooms, quartered
½ cup chopped onion
½ cup butter
2 tablespoons flour
2 tablespoons fresh snipped dill
  or 3-4 tablespoons dry dill
1 cup chicken broth

1 cup heavy cream
Juice of 1 lemon
Salt and pepper to taste
2 tablespoons dry white wine
2 pounds shrimp, cooked
  and deveined
4 cups cooked rice

Preheat oven to 325 degrees. Saute mushrooms and onions in butter over medium heat. Stir in flour and dill, mixing well. Add broth and cream. Bring to a boil slowly. Add lemon juice, salt, pepper, and wine. Reduce heat and simmer until sauce thickens; add shrimp and simmer until well blended. Put steamed rice in bottom of buttered 13x9x2 inch baking dish. Pour shrimp mixture over rice. Bake 15 minutes. Do not overcook.

Yield: 8 serving

## CRAWFISH DELIGHT

1 pound cooked crawfish tails
½ stick butter
3 tablespoons flour
1 medium onion, minced
2 cloves garlic, minced

2 tablespoons parsley, minced
½ cup green onion, chopped
½ cup white wine
1 cup heavy cream
Salt, pepper, paprika, to taste

Melt butter, add flour and blend well. Add next four ingredients; saute until tender. Add crawfish and simmer 10 minutes. Add wine, blending well. Slowly stir in cream and simmer over low heat. Add seasonings and heat. Serve on toastpoints or in patty shells.

Yield: 4 servings

## CRAWFISH FETTUCCINI

1 stick butter
1 large onion, chopped
1 rib celery, chopped
1 medium bell pepper, chopped
1 clove garlic, diced
½ pound fresh mushrooms, sliced
1 pound crawfish tails

1½ tablespoons flour
⅔ cup Half & Half
8 ounces Jalapeno Cheez Whiz
2 tablespoons dried parsley
12 ounces fettuccini or egg noodles
Parmesan and Romano cheese,
grated, to taste

Saute vegetables in butter until tender. Add mushrooms and simmer five minutes. Add crawfish and cook for 10 minutes. Stir in flour, blending well. Add Half & Half and Cheez Whiz. Simmer on low heat for 20 minutes, stirring occasionally. Stir cooked noodles into crawfish mixture and mix well. Pour into casserole and top with Parmesan and Romano cheeses. Bake in 350 degree oven for 20 minutes.

Yield: 4-6 servings

## CRAWFISH PIE

1 stick margarine
5 tablespoons flour
1½-2 cups milk
Cayenne pepper, to taste
1 cup green onion tops, chopped
¼ bell pepper, chopped fine

3 tablespoons dry sherry (optional)
Cajun or Creole Seasoning,
to taste
1 tablespoon garlic puree
2 pounds crawfish tails
1 can chopped mushrooms, drained
24 small pie shells

In heavy skillet, saute onion and bell pepper in margarine. Blend in flour well and add milk slowly; season with cayenne. Simmer on low heat until thickened. Add remaining ingredients. Mix well, adjust seasonings for flavor, and place in pie shells. Bake pies in 375 degree oven for 30 minutes until filling is hot and bubbly.

Yield: 24 small pies

# CRABMEAT AU GRATIN

*My predictable husband orders this dish every time we eat in a seafood restaurant. He scans the menu for a long time with his glasses perched on the end of his nose, slaps the menu shut and declares, "I think I'll have the Crabmeat au Gratin." No kidding!*

| | |
|---|---|
| 1 stick butter | 1 teaspoon white pepper |
| ½ cup onion, chopped fine | 2 squirts Tabasco |
| ¼ cup celery, chopped fine | 1 (14 ounce) can evaporated milk |
| ¼ cup flour | ¼ cup dry white wine |
| 1 teaspoon salt | 8 ounces grated mild Cheddar |
| 1 pound lump crabmeat | |

Saute onions and celery in butter until tender. Add flour gradually and stir until smooth. Add evaporated milk slowly, blending well and stirring constantly to prevent lumps. Add egg yolk, salt, red pepper and Tabasco. Cook, stirring, about 15 minutes. Blend in wine. Gently fold in crabmeat and place in lightly greased baking dish. Sprinkle with cheese. Bake in 375 degree oven for about 30 minutes until hot and bubbly.

Yield: 4-6 servings

# DONNA'S CRAB STUFFED POTATOES

*My daughter Donna shared this recipe with me — it is truly succulent!*

| | |
|---|---|
| 6 large baking potatoes | 2 teaspoons salt |
| 1 pound lump crabmeat | 8 teaspoons grated onion |
| 1 cup butter | 2 cups sharp grated Cheddar |
| ¾ cup milk | Paprika for topping |

Bake potatoes, remove from skins, reserving skins for filling. Mash potatoes until smooth, with butter and milk. Add salt, grated onion and Cheddar. Fold in crabmeat. Fill potato skins and sprinkle with paprika. Bake in 350 degree oven until hot and bubbly.

Yield: 12 servings

# CRABMEAT AND ARTICHOKE DIVINE

6 tablespoons butter
6 tablespoons flour
3 cups milk
Salt and white pepper, to taste
½ teaspoon Worcestershire
1 cup grated Parmesan, divided

½ teaspoon dry mustard
¼ teaspoon Tabasco
4 hard boiled eggs, chopped
2 cans artichoke hearts,
    packed in water
2 pounds lump crabmeat

Make a cream sauce of butter and flour, gradually adding milk and stirring constantly.  Season with salt, white pepper, Worcestershire, mustard, Tabasco and one-half cup Parmesan.  Add the eggs and simmer on low heat until the mixture thickens.  Coat individual casserole dishes with butter.  Place a portion of the crabmeat in the dishes and top with sauce. Nestle 2 or 3 whole artichoke hearts in each dish and top with remaining Parmesan.  Bake at 350 degrees for 15 minutes until hot and bubbly. Delicious served with a broiled tomato.

Yield:  6 servings

# CRAB PATTIES

1½ tubes buttery crackers,
    finely crushed, divided
½ onion, finely chopped
½ cup green onion tops, chopped
1 egg

¼ cup milk (approximate)
1 teaspoon Old Bay Seasoning
Garlic powder, cayenne and salt,
    to taste
½ pound lump crabmeat

Mix 1 tube buttery crackers with onions.  Add egg which has been beaten with milk.  Toss in crabmeat lightly and add garlic powder, Old Bay seasoning and salt.  Shape into patties and roll in one-half tube crushed crackers.  Fry on medium-high heat in small amount oil for about 8 minutes on each side.  Drain well and serve.

Yield:  8-10 patties

## SIMPLE STUFFED CRAB

*These are light, delicious and chock-full of fresh lump crabmeat.*

| | |
|---|---|
| 3 sticks margarine | 1 cup milk |
| 3 onions, chopped | Cayenne pepper, to taste |
| 1 bell pepper, chopped | Salt, to taste |
| 4 stalks celery, chopped | 4 pounds lump crabmeat |
| 1 bunch green onion tops, chopped | 1 cup prepared bread crumbs |
| 8 slices stale white bread | Dots of margarine (for top) |

Saute vegetables in margarine until tender. Toast bread in 250 degree oven to dry; soak in milk until all milk is saturated. Add bread to vegetable mixture, blending well. Add cayenne pepper and salt; fold in crabmeat. Pile mixture lightly into shells or ramekins; top with bread crumbs and dots of margarine. Bake in 350 degree oven for 20-30 minutes.

Yield: 25-30 stuffed crabs (Approximate)


## SOUTHERN OYSTER PIE

| | |
|---|---|
| 1 pint oysters | ½ teaspoon salt and cayenne |
| 6 slices bacon | ¼ cup parsley, chopped |
| ½ pound fresh sliced mushrooms | 2 tablespoons lemon juice |
| ½ cup onion, chopped | 2 squirts Tabasco |
| ½ cup green onion, chopped | Prepared biscuit dough |
| ¼ cup flour | |

Drain oysters and check for shell. Fry bacon and crumble, reserving three tablespoons drippings. Add next three ingredients to reserved bacon grease and simmer 5 minutes. Blend in flour, salt, pepper and Tabasco. Stir in oysters, bacon, parsley, and lemon juice. Place mixture in a greased 9-inch pie plate. Top with biscuit dough. Make several slits in dough. Bake in 400 degree oven for 20-25 minutes, until biscuit dough is golden brown.

Yield: 6 servings

# ED'S HOLIDAY SCALLOPED OYSTERS

*Whatever the menu, my husband prepares this dish for holidays. It has become his most requested dish.*

1 quart oysters
2 cups coarse cracker crumbs
½ cup margarine, melted
½ teaspoon salt

¼ teaspoon cayenne
¾ cups light cream
½ teaspoon Worcestershire
½ cup oyster liquid

Drain oysters, reserving one-half cup liquid, checking carefully for shell. Set aside. Combine crumbs and margarine. In greased 9-inch baking dish, spread one-third crumbs on the bottom. Cover with one-half of the oysters. Sprinkle lightly with salt and pepper. Repeat layers. Combine cream, Worcestershire, and oyster liquid; pour over layers. Top with crumbs. Bake in 375 degree oven for 30 minutes.

Yield: 6 servings


# OYSTERS BIENVILLE

4 dozen oysters
1 pound cooked shrimp, minced
½ pound fresh mushrooms, minced
2 tablespoons garlic puree
1 large onion, minced
1 stick butter
4 tablespoons flour

1½ cups milk
½ cup heavy cream
1½ cups chicken broth
¼ cup white wine
Grated Parmesan, to taste
½ cup bread crumbs
Paprika, to taste

Melt butter, blend in flour; add milk, cream, broth and wine. Stir until thickened. Add shrimp, mushrooms, garlic and onion and simmer slowly about 20 minutes. Place oysters in shells on rock salt and place under broiler for 2-3 minutes. Drain off liquid. Cover with sauce, grated Parmesan, bread crumbs and paprika. Broil until hot and bubbly.

Yield: 4 servings

# OYSTERS ROCKEFELLER MONETTE STYLE

4 dozen oysters and shells
1 bunch green onions
1 stalk celery
1 bunch fresh parsley
2 pkgs. frozen spinach, cooked
and drained well
1 pound butter, melted
¼ teaspoon anise seed

1 cup bread crumbs
2 ounces Worcestershire sauce
1 ounce Absinthe
Salt, to taste
Black and cayenne pepper, to taste
1 teaspoon anchovy paste
½ cup Parmesan cheese

Grind all vegetables in a food processor, using melted butter as liquid. Add anise seed, bread crumbs, Worcestershire, absinthe, salt and peppers and anchovy paste. Blend in Parmesan cheese, reserving some for topping. Place oysters in half shells and place on a large pan with rock salt. Place under broiler for about 5 minutes; remove from oven and pour liquid from each shell. Cover each oyster with Rockefeller Sauce, sprinkle with reserved Parmesan and put back under broiler until hot and bubbly. Serve immediately.

Yield: 4 servings

# BROILED BROCHETTE

2 dozen large shrimp, deveined
2 dozen large oysters, drained
6 slices lean bacon, cut in half
1 stick butter, melted

12 large fresh mushrooms, cut in
quarters or thickly sliced
Tabasco, Cajun seasoning, to taste
1 teaspoon fresh lemon juice

Wrap one shrimp and one oyster in one-half slice lean bacon and secure with toothpick. Repeat with all shrimp, oysters and bacon. Place brochettes and mushrooms on a large baking pan; drizzle with melted butter, lemon, and sprinkle with Tabasco and Cajun seasoning. Broil about 15 minutes until bacon is crisp or place on heavy duty foil and cook over hot coals.

Yield: 24 brochettes

*Carol Ann Daniel*

# *Veggies/Sides*

It won't take you long to realize as you thumb through this chapter that I like my vegetables "enhanced". Steamed veggies, where we are allowed to "savor the simple flavor", are definitely not my style. Give me my mustard or turnip greens filled with salt meat and hot pepper vinegar, my broccoli drizzled with hollandaise, and my cauliflower dripping with cheese!

When it comes to fresh versus frozen or canned, I am adamant about using nothing but fresh mushrooms and fresh asparagus. There is simply no comparing the difference in flavor, texture and appearance of the two. On the other hand, I use nothing but frozen baby limas, and think nothing of purchasing canned green beans. I am a true believer that it's all in the preparation!

A southern cook seasons with a magic touch that sets her vegetables apart. This gal can turn a simple baked onion or tomato into a work of art. She can season smothered okra and tomatoes to transform a meal into a feast. My Mom never apologized for cooking her green beans to death, but, if she had a mind to, she could cook them as crunchy as the most sophisticated chef, and garnish them in many ways such as hollandaise or almondine sauce.

The side dishes that I feature in this chapter, such as potatoes, rice, and dressings, are also to-die-for good, with most of them simple to prepare and easy to make ahead. I hope that you will get as much enjoyment serving these delicious dishes to your family and friends as I have over the years.

## ARTICHOKE HEART CASSEROLE

*If you're looking for a different vegetable casserole, give this a try. It is an excellent accompaniment to light Italian dishes, such as Veal Scallopini.*

¼ cup olive oil
4 cans artichoke hearts
2 tablespoons minced onion
1 teaspoon garlic puree
Salt, to taste

Cayenne pepper, to taste
½ cup dry white wine
1 cup Parmesan cheese, grated
²/₃ cup mozzarella cheese, grated
1½ cups seasoned bread crumbs

Grease casserole with olive oil. Cut artichoke hearts into quarters. Mix all remaining ingredients except bread crumbs. Place in a two-quart casserole, sprinkle with bread crumbs and bake in 350 degree oven for 30-40 minutes.

Yield: 6 servings

## HOLIDAY CORN CASSEROLE

*If ever there was a classic holiday vegetable dish, this is it! This make-ahead casserole is also the perfect offering for a pot luck dinner.*

2 cans creamed corn
2 eggs, beaten
¾ cups yellow cornmeal
¾ tablespoon garlic puree
¼ cup Crisco oil
1 large onion, chopped

2 Jalapenos, chopped and seeded
1 small jar diced pimentos
½ pound medium cheddar, grated
12 saltine crackers, crushed
1 stick margarine, melted

Mix together the first nine ingredients, blending well. Place in a greased three-quart baking dish. Top with crushed crackers; pour melted margarine over crackers. Bake uncovered in 400 degree oven for 35-40 minutes, until hot and bubbly.

Yield: 8-10 servings

## SHOEPEG CORN CASSEROLE

*This recipe is courtesy of my former neighbor and dear friend, Sarah Harrison. Sarah and her husband Dick, who passed away in the summer of '98, were long-time friends with whom we had many fun sessions creating dishes and trading secrets in the kitchen.*

1 (8 ounce) pkg. cream cheese
¼ cup milk
2 tablespoons margarine
1 small white onion, chopped

2 cans shoepeg corn, drained
1 can chopped green chilis
⅔ cup plain bread crumbs
Paprika, to taste

Heat cream cheese and milk, and blend well. Saute onion in margarine and blend in cream cheese/milk mixture. Add drained corn and chilis. Mix well. Place in two-quart casserole and top with bread crumbs and paprika. Bake in 325 degree oven until hot and bubbly, about 30 minutes.

Yield: 4-6 servings

## TO-DIE-FOR CORN FRITTERS

*I once catered an old-fashioned picnic-style party featuring country food, complete with fried chicken and the works. Our Corn Fritters were the hit of the evening — light and bursting with flavor!*

1 cup flour
¼ cup sugar
1 teaspoon baking powder
1 teaspoon salt
½ teaspoon white pepper

½ teaspoon cayenne pepper
1 egg, beaten
3 cups canned corn, drained well
3 tablespoons whipping cream
1 tablespoon butter, melted

Combine flour, sugar, baking powder, salt, white pepper and cayenne pepper in a mixing bowl; blend well. Combine egg, corn, whipping cream, and butter; mix well and stir into dry ingredients. Drop mixture by tablespoons into hot oil (375 degrees); fry until golden brown, turning once. Drain on paper towels. Serve piping hot.

Yield: 2-3 dozen

# THE BEST BAKED BEANS IN THE SOUTH

*Another winning recipe, courtesy of my husband, Ed, who loves simple, easy-to-prepare dishes. Be sure to allow plenty of baking time, since the secret to tender beans is in the slow baking.*

1 (16-20 ounce) can
    Campbells Pork & Beans
¼ cup brown sugar

¼ cup ketchup
4-5 lean bacon slices

Mix beans, brown sugar and catsup. Place in 1½-quart casserole dish. Cover with bacon slices. Bake uncovered in 275 degree oven for 1½-2 hours, until tender.

Yield:  4 servings

# TOMATOES/SPINACH SUPREME

*The combination of tomato and spinach in this dish is not only colorful, but pleasing to the palate as well. A beautiful dish for a buffet dinner!*

4 large tomatoes
Garlic salt, to taste
Pepper, to taste
3 (10 ounce) pkgs. frozen
    chopped spinach
½ cup plain bread crumbs, divided
4 stalks green onion tops, chopped

2 tablespoons butter, melted
1½ teaspoons salt
½ cup Parmesan, grated, divided
½ teaspoon garlic puree
½ teaspoon thyme, crumbled
2 eggs, beaten lightly

Slice each tomato into three big chunks and sprinkle with pepper and garlic salt. Place slices on a buttered baking dish. Cook spinach, using package directions; drain well in a colander, squeezing out all moisture. Mix spinach with remaining ingredients, reserving one-fourth cup bread crumbs and one-fourth cup Parmesan for top. Spoon mixture on top of each tomato slice and shape it into a mound. Sprinkle with remaining bread crumbs and Parmesan. Bake uncovered in 375 degree oven for 20-25 minutes.

Yield:  6-8 servings

# GREEN BEAN/BROCCOLI CASSEROLE

1 pkg. frozen, chopped broccoli
2 cans cut green beans, drained
Salt and pepper, to taste
¾ cup sharp cheddar, grated

1 can cream of mushroom soup
1 can French fried onions, divided
1 can water chestnuts, drained
1 can sliced mushrooms, drained

Slice water chestnuts; set aside. Cook broccoli and green beans in water with salt and pepper for 5 minutes; drain and toss with grated cheese. Blend in remaining ingredients, reserving some onion rings for topping. Place in greased two-quart casserole dish and bake uncovered in 375 degree oven for 30 minutes until hot and bubbly. Remove from oven, top with onion rings and return to oven for 3 minutes.

Yield: 6 servings

# ITALIAN BEAN CASSEROLE

3 cans Italian green beans
1 pound lean bacon
2 medium onions, chopped
1 teaspoon garlic puree
½ cup water

Cayenne and salt, to taste
Tabasco, to taste
1 can cream of mushroom soup
¾ cup Parmesan cheese
⅔ cup Italian bread crumbs

Drain beans; set aside. Fry bacon until crisp; cool and crumble coarsely and set aside. Saute chopped onions and garlic puree in about one-third of the bacon drippings. Add the water to sauteed onions and season with cayenne pepper, salt and Tabasco. Cover pot and let simmer about 10 minutes. Blend mushroom soup into this mixture. Place drained green beans and bacon in a large mixing bowl and pour soup mixture over beans. Add Parmesan and mix well. Pour beans into a casserole dish and sprinkle top with bread crumbs. Bake uncovered in 350 degree oven until hot and bubbly, about 30 minutes.

Yield: 12 servings

## GOURMET GREEN BEANS IN BACON

*Words fail me in describing this dish. What can I say — it is different, it is tasty, it is attractive, it goes with everything, it can be made ahead... I could go on and on! This dish is especially wonderful served with barbecued or smoked meats.*

2 cans vertical pack whole
  green beans

6-8 slices lean bacon
½ cup Kraft barbecue sauce

Using four at a time, wrap green beans in one-half slice bacon until all green beans are wrapped. Line bean bundles in a sprayed, shallow baking dish. Drizzle barbecue sauce on each bunch of beans. Bake uncovered in a 350 degree oven for 45 minutes. Pour off drippings and serve. (Regular whole green beans can be used if vertical pack is unavailable.)

Yield: 4-6 servings

## FRENCH BEANS ALMONDINE

4 slices lean bacon
1 small onion, chopped
1 teaspoon garlic puree
2 cans French style
  green beans, drained

²/₃ cup water
1 teaspoon sugar
1 teaspoon cider vinegar
Salt and pepper, to taste
½ cup sliced almonds, toasted

Fry bacon, drain and crumble coarsely. In bacon grease, saute minced onion and garlic. Add drained green beans and remaining ingredients, except almonds. Cover and simmer green beans on low heat for about 30 minutes. Drain and toss with almonds to serve.

Yield: 4-6 servings

*I have found when using canned green beans, they are tastier when I drain off the liquid and cook them in fresh water.*

## EDWIN'S SHERRIED CARROTS

*Several years ago my husband decided to pitch in and help cook for a dinner party. We had veal, wild rice, carrots, salad and fluffy rolls. This was his contribution and it has been a favorite ever since. Even carrot haters love this succulent dish. This man will find a recipe on a can, a bag of veggies, or a coupon and turn it into a gourmet dish!*

| | |
|---|---|
| 1 (1 pound) bag frozen whole | ¼ teaspoon ground cloves |
|    baby carrots | ¼ cup margarine, melted |
| 1 cup water | ¼ teaspoon salt |
| 1 can whole small onions, drained | 1 tablespoon cream sherry |
| ¹/₃ cup brown sugar, firmly packed | |

Cook carrots in salted water for 15 minutes; drain well. Place carrots and drained onions in two-quart greased casserole. For glaze, melt margarine in a saucepan and add remaining ingredients. When well blended, pour over vegetables in casserole. Bake uncovered in 400 degree oven for 30 minutes. Toss lightly before serving to evenly distribute glaze.

Yield: 6 servings

## SMOTHERED CARROTS

| | |
|---|---|
| 1 pound fresh, whole carrots | 1 teaspoon garlic puree |
| 1 stick margarine | Salt and pepper to taste |
| 1 large onion, chopped | 3 tablespoons brown sugar |
| 2 stalks celery, chopped | 1 tablespoon brandy (optional) |

Scrape and cut carrots in one-inch pieces. Melt margarine in heavy skillet and add onion and celery. Let simmer about five minutes and add carrots, garlic puree, and salt and pepper. Let simmer uncovered about 30 minutes. Blend in brown sugar and brandy; cover skillet and simmer on low heat for about 15 additional minutes.

Yield: 4-6 servings

# SMOTHERED OKRA PODS

*This is a simple and delicious way to prepare okra. I love it because there is virtually no <u>slime</u>, as there is with boiled okra. I have reached the conclusion that it's the water that makes okra slimy! Simmering the okra pods slowly in margarine gives them a golden/crisp outside — Yummy!*

20 fresh, small whole okra pods or   ½ stick butter or margarine
   1 box frozen whole baby okra   Salt and pepper, to taste

Melt margarine or butter in large skillet. Add whole okra pods in one layer. Smother, uncovered, on low heat until the okra pods are golden brown and tender, rolling them around in the butter now and then to brown evenly.

Yield: 4 servings

# SOUTHERN OKRA AND TOMATOES

*The blending of okra and tomatoes provides hearty nourishment for a family dinner. Add onion, bell pepper and bacon and you've got a winner. To really knock your socks off, add one pound peeled raw shrimp when you add the tomatoes — magnificent!*

3 slices lean bacon   1 medium onion, chopped
2 pounds fresh baby okra,   ½ medium bell pepper, chopped
   sliced thin   1 (15 ounce) can diced tomatoes,
Salt and pepper, to taste      drain and reserve liquid
3 tablespoons cider vinegar

Fry bacon in heavy iron Dutch oven; drain and crumble. Place okra in bacon drippings, add salt and pepper, cider vinegar, and simmer uncovered until slime cooks out. Add onions, bell pepper and drained tomatoes. Simmer uncovered about 15 minutes, stirring often. Add reserved liquid from tomatoes and reserved crumbled bacon and blend well. Cover and simmer over low heat, stirring often, for 40-45 minutes until okra is tender.

Yield: 6 servings

## MAY-MAY'S TURNIPS AND SAUSAGE

*I tasted this Cajun lady's food while visiting a hunting camp in Cameron, Louisiana many years ago. May-May cooked for "starving" hunters each and every day. I will never forget that meal — roast duck, venison, fried chicken, rice and gravy (naturally) and a melange of the best vegetables, homemade breads, and desserts I have ever tasted. I served myself a sizeable portion of this sausage and "potatoes" and soon went back for more. Imagine my surprise to learn that I had eaten my first turnips!*

6-8 medium fresh turnips          1 large onion, chopped
1 pound smoked sausage          ¼ cup water

Cut turnips in one-half inch cubes; set aside. Cut smoked sausage into one-half inch cubes. In heavy black iron Dutch oven, saute sausage pieces until browned; add turnips and onions and blend well. Let simmer uncovered for 15 minutes on low heat. Blend in water, cover, and simmer about 30-40 minutes until sausage is done and turnips are tender. Stir often.

Yield: 6-8 servings

## NONNON YEAGLEY'S TURNIPS

*My husband's Grandmother was reputed to be one of the best cooks in Shreveport. These turnips will attest to that!*

6-8 medium fresh turnips          Salt and pepper, to taste
1-2 quarts water          ½ cup Half & Half
1½ teaspoons sugar          ½ cup sharp cheddar, grated

Cut turnips into two inch chunks and place in heavy saucepan with water, sugar, and salt. Boil turnips until tender, about 20-30 minutes. Drain turnips and place in a two-quart casserole. Toss with Half & Half and pepper; sprinkle with cheese. Keep warm until ready to serve.

Yield: 4-6 servings

## CHEESY SQUASH BAKE

1 pound baby yellow squash
¼ cup red bell pepper, chopped
½ cup mayonnaise

½ cup mild cheddar, shredded
¼ cup chopped green onion tops
1 egg white, beaten until stiff

Place whole squash in a saucepan with a little salted water and steam for 15 minutes, until crisp-tender; drain and slice. In nine-inch pie plate place squash and red bell pepper, reserving one tablespoon bell pepper for garnish. Combine mayonnaise with grated cheese and green onion, reserving 2 tablespoons cheese for topping. Fold in beaten egg whites. Spread over squash, covering well. Bake in 350 degree oven for 20-30 minutes until hot and bubbly. Sprinkle reserved bell pepper and cheese on top and return to oven for 2-3 minutes to melt cheese.

Yield: 4 servings

Note: Squash can be substituted with 2 cans cut asparagus, well drained. (Do not steam before placing in casserole dish.) Delicious!

## SQUASH PUFFS

2 cups fresh yellow squash, grated
½ teaspoon salt
¼ cup, plus 2 tablespoons flour
2 teaspoons onion, finely chopped

2 teaspoons sugar
¼ teaspoon black pepper
2 eggs, beaten
4 tablespoons margarine

Combine squash, onion, sugar, salt and pepper. Cover and let stand 30 minutes. Drain thoroughly. Add flour and eggs and blend well. Melt margarine in large skillet over medium heat. Drop squash mixture by tablespoons into hot margarine. Let simmer until golden brown, turning once.

Yield: 6-8 servings

# BROCCOLI CASSEROLE

*This is an old recipe, with many variations. It is as delightful now as it was 30 years ago.*

½ stick margarine
1 large onion, chopped
½ cup celery
½ pound fresh mushrooms, sliced
3 pkgs. chopped frozen broccoli,
   drained well

1 roll garlic cheese, cut in cubes
1 can cream of mushroom soup
1 pkg. sliced almonds
1 can sliced water chestnuts
½ cup plain breadcrumbs

Saute onions, celery and mushrooms in margarine. Blend in remaining ingredients, except breadcrumbs. Place in a two-quart casserole, cover with breadcrumbs and bake uncovered in 350 degree oven for 40 minutes, until hot and bubbly.

Yield: 6 servings

# THE ULTIMATE ASPARAGUS CASSEROLE

*This simple-to-make dish is, without a doubt, my favorite company vegetable dish. It is sophisticated in both taste and presentation, and brings out the best flavors in any accompanying dishes. I have seen people who "hate" asparagus go back for seconds.*

2 cans cut asparagus, drained well
1 (10 ounce) can
   cream of celery soup

White pepper, to taste
½ cup mild cheddar cheese, grated
1 can French fried onion rings

Place drained asparagus in one-quart shallow baking dish or pie plate. Spread soup evenly over asparagus. Sprinkle with white pepper and grated cheese. Bake in 350 degree oven for 30 minutes, until hot and bubbly. Remove from oven and cover with French fried onion rings. Return to oven for five minutes. Serve immediately while onion rings are crispy and dish is piping hot.

Yield: 6 servings

## NONNON YEAGLEY'S YAMS

*This recipe of my husband's grandmother is a favorite in our home. Nonnon's memory lives on every Thanksgiving when I place those piping hot yams on the table.*

| | |
|---|---|
| 6 medium sweet potatoes | ½ teaspoon cinnamon |
| Water to cover | ⅛ teaspoon ground cloves |
| Dash salt | 1⅛ teaspoons nutmeg |
| 2 eggs, well beaten | ½ cup chopped pecans |
| ¼ cup sugar | ½ cup Half & Half |
| ¼ cup margarine | 1 small bag mini marshmallows |
| ½ teaspoon salt | |

Boil potatoes in lightly salted water until tender. Peel and mash well. Add remaining ingredients except marshmallows and mix well. Place in 2 quart casserole and bake in 375 degree oven for 40 minutes. Remove from oven and place marshmallows on top; return to oven and bake until marshmallows are golden and fluffy.

Yield: 8 servings

## BAKED SWEET POTATOES

*The plain baked sweet potato, simple as it is, is still our favorite.*

2 medium to large sweet potatoes     Butter or margarine, to taste

Wash and dry sweet potatoes. Grease each potato with oil or shortening and place on baking pan lined with foil. Bake in 400 degree oven for about one hour, until fork tender. Remove from oven, peel, and slather with butter. Serve immediately.

Yield: 2 servings

Note: If potatoes are done before the rest of your meal, place them in a brown paper bag, and forget them. When it's time to serve them, the peels come off very easily.

# SIMPLE YAM AND APPLE CASSEROLE

*This is a layer-and-bake recipe. Simple and delicious, this was my very first yam recipe as a young bride! The pecans add a touch of class!*

1 large can yams, reserve juice
2 large red Delicious apples
¼ cup granulated sugar
Cinnamon and nutmeg, to taste
½ cup honey

½ cup pecan halves
1 stick butter
1 small bag miniature
   marshmallows

Cut yams and apples into medium-sized pieces and place with pecan halves in one layer, in a 13x9x2 inch baking dish. Dot liberally with butter. Sprinkle with sugar, cinnamon and nutmeg. Drizzle honey over all and carefully pour a little of the yam juice for added moisture. Bake uncovered in 325 degree oven for one hour. Remove from oven, add marshmallows and return for five minutes, until golden.

Yield: 6-8 servings


# SARAH'S GLAZED YAMS

*Thanks go to my dear friend Sarah Harrison for this delicious recipe!*

4 large sweet potatoes
1 cup sugar
1 teaspoon cinnamon
Dash nutmeg

2 tablespoons flour
½ stick margarine, melted
¼ cup water

Combine sugar, cinnamon, nutmeg and flour. Add melted margarine and water and blend well. Place in saucepan and bring to a boil. Peel sweet potatoes and cut lengthwise, like French fries. Pour mixture over cut sweet potatoes that have been placed in 13x9x2 inch casserole dish. Bake uncovered in a 375 degree oven for 30-40 minutes, until yams are tender. The potatoes will have a glazed appearance. Easy and delicious!

Yield: 6-8 servings

## DAWN'S STUFFED BAKED POTATO

*Thanks for this one go to my precious little friend, Dawn Barnett. Many hours we spent cooking together — many holidays we shared!*

| | |
|---|---|
| 4 large baking potatoes | 4-5 green onion tops, chopped |
| 6 slices lean bacon | 8-10 ounces Velveeta, cut in cubes |
| 1 stick BUTTER, cut in cubes | Salt and black pepper, to taste |
| 8 ounces sour cream | 4 ounces cheddar, grated |

Bake potatoes until tender. Fry bacon until crisp, cool and crumble; set aside. When potatoes are tender, cut each in half, scoop out potato carefully to prevent tearing skins. In a large bowl, combine potato and butter and beat with electric mixer. Blend in bacon, sour cream, onions, Velveeta, salt and pepper. Place potato filling back in skins and sprinkle with cheddar. At this point, potatoes can be placed in refrigerator until ready to bake. Bake in 375 degree oven for 20 minutes, until stuffing is hot and bubbly.

Yield: 8 servings

## HASH BROWN CASSEROLE

| | |
|---|---|
| 1 (2 pound) bag frozen hash browns, thawed | 1 pint sour cream |
| 1 large onion, chopped | 8 ounces Velveeta, cut in cubes |
| Salt and pepper, to taste | 6 slices lean bacon, fried and crumbled (optional) |
| 1½ sticks margarine, divided | 1 tube buttery crackers, coarsely crushed |
| 1 can cream of chicken soup | |

In large bowl mix hash browns, onions, salt and pepper. Melt margarine and blend one-half into potato mixture. In heavy saucepan, mix soup, sour cream and Velveeta; blend well and heat, stirring until Velveeta is melted. Blend mixture into potatoes, add bacon, and place in greased 15x10x3 inch casserole. Mix reserved melted margarine with crackers and sprinkle on potatoes. Bake in 325 degree oven for one hour.

Yield: 12 servings

## DEBBIE'S BROCCOLI RICE

*Although I have tried many Broccoli Rice recipes, my daughter Debbie's remains our favorite. Daughters are wonderful!*

1 stick margarine
1 cup onion, chopped
1 cup celery, chopped
½ pound fresh mushrooms, sliced
1 small jar Jalapeno Cheese Whiz
   cut in small chunks

2 (10 ounce) pkg. frozen, chopped
   broccoli, thawed and drained
1 can cream of chicken soup
1 can cream of mushroom soup
3 cups cooked rice
1 can sliced water chestnuts

Melt margarine in large skillet and saute onion and celery until tender. Add mushrooms and saute another five minutes. Blend in Cheese Whiz and stir over low heat until melted. Add thawed and drained chopped broccoli, then soups. Fold in cooked rice and sliced water chestnuts; toss well. Place in greased casserole dish and bake uncovered in 350 degree oven for 35-40 minutes.

Yield: 8-10 servings

## SHRIMP RICE

1 stick margarine
2 pounds peeled raw shrimp
6 green onions, chopped
1 stalk celery, chopped
¼ bell pepper, chopped
Salt and pepper, to taste

1 cup raw long-grained rice
   (preferably Uncle Ben's)
1 can cream of mushroom soup
1 cup water
½ cup dry white wine

In heavy skillet, saute shrimp in margarine until pink. Sprinkle lightly with salt and pepper. Add onion, celery and bell pepper, rice, soup, water and wine. Mix well. Cover skillet tightly and simmer for 20-25 minutes, until rice is tender. Toss lightly and serve.

Yield: 4-6 servings

# RICE WITH WATER CHESTNUTS AND MUSHROOMS

*This recipe lends itself to any meat — pork, chicken, venison, duck, beef. The crunch of the water chestnuts adds a little something extra!*

½ pound fresh mushrooms, sliced
1 can sliced water chestnuts
1¼ cups raw long-grain rice

1 stick margarine
1 can French onion soup
⅔ cup water

Drain can of water chestnuts, reserving liquid. Melt margarine in skillet; add rice and stir over medium heat until golden. Stir in water chestnuts and mushrooms and saute until well blended. Add soup, liquid from water chestnuts, water and a dash of salt. Pour mixture into sprayed two-quart casserole; cover and bake in 350 degree oven for one hour. Toss lightly and serve.

Yield: 6 servings

# LEMON-DILL RICE

*One holiday several years ago, my husband's talented daughter Susan made us a pretty gift basket filled with a unique and diverse assortment of goodies. One such goodie was Lemon-Dill Rice Mix. The dry ingredients were in a little bag, tied with a colorful ribbon which held the recipe. How delicious it was served with roasted pork tenderloin!*

1 cup raw rice
1½ teaspoons dried lemon peel
1 teaspoon dillweed
½ teaspoon dried chives

½ teaspoon salt
2 chicken bouillon cubes
2 cups cold water
1 tablespoon butter

Combine first 6 ingredients with water and butter in a heavy sauce pan. Turn heat high and bring to a boil. Reduce heat to medium-low, stir once with a fork and cover tightly. Simmer for about 15 minutes or until all liquid is absorbed.

Yield: 4-6 servings

# JANE'S OYSTER DRESSING

*This marvelous dressing is the creation of a dear friend of many years, Jane Barnett. Jane hails from South Louisiana where entertaining in the home is still very much in fashion, and the kitchen is the gathering place. In Jane and Billy's home, every room is a "hearth" room where you'll find genuine Southern hospitality. The relaxed, laid-back atmosphere makes visitors feel welcome, while the innovative, delicious meals that Jane prepares are guaranteed to be a culinary treat. Some of my fondest memories of long ago are of Friday evenings at Jane's where friends gathered in her warm and inviting kitchen, sipping cocktails and watching her put the finishing touches on a huge pot of seafood gumbo or crawfish etouffee. Jane is the only person I've ever known who could turn frying shrimp into a community affair — an art! To this day, I can picture her battering and frying, a few shrimp at a time, until the platter was heaped with golden, crispy fried shrimp. What pageantry! This gal could make mud cakes taste like filet mignon — and enjoy doing it! I hope you'll try Jane's Oyster Dressing — it is truly outstanding! It's simple to prepare and can be made a day ahead. One word of advice: don't tamper with the recipe — it cannot be improved on!*

1 pound Jimmy Dean regular bulk
   sausage, crumbled
1 pint oysters, drained (cut in half
   if large), reserve liquid
½ cup fresh parsley, minced
½ cup green onion tops, chopped

4 hamburger buns, dried in low
   oven and crumbled coarsely
4 tablespoons margarine, melted
Juice of ½ lemon
¼ cup bread crumbs
   (approximately)

Brown sausage in a lightly greased fry pan. Add oysters, parsley and green onion tops, and cook for 10 minutes. Stir in crumbled buns, margarine and lemon juice. Blend well and add oyster liquid if stuffing is not moist enough. Place mixture in greased baking dish. Lightly sprinkle bread crumbs on top and dot with a little margarine. Bake, uncovered, at 325 degrees for about 30 minutes, until hot and bubbly.

Yield: 6 servings

*Sara Grace
Daniel*

# Breakfast/Brunch

The art of the brunch!! The quiet of morning, broken by laughter and the clinking of glasses, the delicate staccato of silver against china. A table laden with great slabs of Virginia ham, sausage links, crisp lean bacon, quiches, omelets, fluffy biscuits, hot steaming grits, a tureen filled with steaming oyster bisque, a crisp spinach salad dotted with fresh raspberries, orange slices and almonds, and a colorful array of fresh fruit on a silver tray.

Brunch, which is usually served buffet-style, is basically a late breakfast, with a little more food and pageantry than a regular breakfast. It is my favorite mode of entertaining, and this late morning festivity can turn any event into an occasion — weddings, holidays, sporting events, card parties. The ideas for menus are limitless, from a rib-sticking, heart warming breakfast with grits, eggs, and the works, to a fancy soiree with dainty crepes, fancy souffles, and tiny finger desserts.

As for beverages, the variety is endless — an assortment of juices, coffee, capuccino, milk punches, Mimosas, Bellinis, and Bloody Marys. I believe the proper term for all this abundance is *decadence!*

Since brunch is our favorite mode of entertaining, it's only fitting that we host several brunches during the spring and holiday seasons. Each and every recipe featured in this chapter has been tested time and time again, so be my guest and sample each and every one.

# SAUSAGE STRATA

*This dish is a tradition, stemming from my South Louisiana days, so many of which were spent with Nadine and Jerry Arbaugh, our closest friends. How many breakfasts did we enjoy, sipping Bloody Marys and feasting on fine food on the veranda of their beautiful riverfront home, the site of our wedding! This strata is from the Arbaughs!*

1 pound Jimmie Dean bulk
   sausage with sage
2-3 slices rye bread, cubed
6 eggs, beaten

1 cup milk
Salt and pepper, to taste
Dash dry mustard and nutmeg
1½ cups grated Swiss or Cheddar

Layer bread cubes, sausage and one-half of cheese in 10 inch square baking dish. Beat eggs with milk, salt, pepper, dry mustard and nutmeg. Pour egg mixture over sausage and add remainder of cheese to the top. If making the day ahead, cover and refrigerate at this point. Bake uncovered in 350 degree oven for 40-45 minutes until set.

Yield: 6 servings

# EGGS GOLDENROD

*This delectable dish is my husband's masterpiece.*

4 hard boiled eggs
2 tablespoons margarine
2 tablespoons flour
1 cup milk

Salt, to taste
4 slices bread
Salt, pepper & paprika,
   for topping

Melt margarine in heavy saucepan, stir in flour, blending well. Add milk slowly and stir until smooth. Cook over medium heat, stirring until it thickens. Add a little salt. Slice egg whites and add to white sauce. Toast bread and lightly butter. Place two bread slices on each individual plate and cover with white sauce. Grate egg yolk over sauce. Sprinkle with salt, pepper and paprika. This is wonderful with fried bacon. Serve immediately.

Yield: 2 servings

# HAM QUICHE

*Another make-ahead family favorite! Simply prepare and bake. Let cool and refrigerate. When ready to serve, pop it in the oven. Freezes well.*

1 unbaked 9-inch pie shell
4 eggs, beaten
1½ cups milk
¼ teaspoon salt

Pepper, to taste
Squirt of Tabasco (optional)
½ pound sharp cheddar, grated
¾ cup diced ham

Combine ingredients. Pour into unbaked pie shell. Bake in 350 degree oven for 45-50 minutes. If making ahead, let cool and refrigerate. To reheat: Cover tightly with foil and heat in 325 degree oven until warm.

Yield: 4 servings

# NEW ORLEANS QUICHE

1 unbaked 9-inch pie shell
1 pound bacon
½ onion, chopped
5 slices cooked ham, diced

5 slices Swiss cheese, cut up
4 eggs, beaten
¾ cup sour cream
Nutmeg, to taste

Fry bacon, and crumble. Saute onions in bacon drippings. Sprinkle crumbled bacon and onions on bottom of pie shell; cover with a layer of ham and a layer of Swiss cheese. Combine beaten eggs and sour cream; pour one-half mixture into pie shell. Layer ham and Swiss cheese; pour remaining egg and sour cream mixture over all. Sprinkle nutmeg over top. Bake in 350 degree oven for 25-30 minutes.

Yield: 6 servings

*Don't throw out leftover Crabmeat Au Gratin.*
*It is perfect for making Crabmeat Omelets*
*for Sunday morning breakfast.*

# CRAB QUICHE

1 unbaked 9-inch pie shell
½ cup mayonnaise
2 tablespoons flour
2 eggs, beaten
½ cup milk

1 can lump crabmeat or
  ½ pound fresh crabmeat
8 ounce Swiss cheese, diced
½ cup green onion, chopped
Salt, pepper & Tabasco, to taste

Combine mayonnaise, flour, eggs and milk. Drain crabmeat and pick over for shells; fold crabmeat, onion and cheese into first mixture. Season to taste with salt, pepper and Tabasco. Pour into pie shell. Bake in 350 degree oven for 40-45 minutes.

Yield: 6 servings

# SPINACH QUICHE

1 unbaked 9-inch pie shell
¼ cup chopped green onion
2 tablespoons margarine
1 pkg. frozen chopped spinach,
  thawed and drained
1 cup shredded Swiss cheese

4 eggs, beaten
1 cup whipping cream
½ cup milk
½ teaspoon salt
½ teaspoon pepper
¼ teaspoon ground nutmeg

Prick the bottom and sides of pie shell with a fork. Bake for 3 minutes in 400 degree oven. Remove from oven and gently prick with fork again. Return shell to oven for an additional 5 minutes. Let cool. While pie shell is cooling, saute onion in butter in a large skillet until tender. Remove from heat and stir in well-drained spinach and cheese. Combine eggs, whipping cream, milk, salt, pepper, and nutmeg in a large mixing bowl. Stir in spinach mixture and mix well. Pour into pastry shell. Bake in a 375 degree oven for 35 minutes or until set. Let stand 10 minutes, cut into wedges and serve.

Yield: 6 servings

## COUNTRY BREAKFAST PIE

*We had this scrumptious pie on a Christmas visit to our daughter Debbie's. Deb's friend, Ginny Still, prepared and delivered these pies as a holiday gift for friends, ready to pop in the oven. Our grandsons Justin and Adam, who love a hearty breakfast, gave this delicious treat a thumbs up! You and your family are guaranteed to love this dish!*

1 pkg. bulk sausage
2 (9-inch) pie shells
1½ cups grated Swiss cheese
4 eggs

¼ cup green bell pepper, chopped
¼ cup red bell pepper, chopped
2 tablespoons chopped onion
1 cup Half and Half

Cook sausage until done; crumble, then drain. Prepare pie shells. (If using Deep Dish pie shells, put all ingredients into one shell.) Mix cheese and sausage. Sprinkle in shells. Lightly beat eggs. Combine remaining ingredients and add to eggs. Pour in shells and bake in 375 degree oven for 40-45 minutes, or until set. Cool on rack for 10 minutes.

Yield: 6 servings

## SAUSAGE DELIGHT

*When my son Danny was young, his friends would appear at our kitchen door before school, knowing full well that I'd open the door and say, "have you kids had breakfast?" I never had to ask twice.*

1 pound Jimmie Dean Hot
   Sausage
1 pound mozzarella cheese
¼ cup green onion tops, chopped

4 eggs, beaten well
Dash Tabasco and Worcestershire
2 pkgs. "Piping Hot White Bread"
   (Dairy Section)

Brown and drain sausage. Add remaining ingredients, except bread, and mix well. Unroll bread dough and add filling in center. Roll bread again and seal edges. Bake in 375 degree oven by baking directions on bread dough package, or until golden brown.

Yield: 6 servings

## SOUTH OF THE BORDER EGGS

*For breakfast/brunch anything goes, so feel free to indulge your appetite. If you're looking for something with a little kick, try this delicious dish with a Southwest flair. All you need to accompany it is a plate full of beautiful fresh fruit, but I'll bet corn muffins would be wonderful also. This dish is also enhanced by Apple Flautas (recipe follows).*

| | |
|---|---|
| 1 cup pitted black olives, halved | 4 eggs |
| 1 cup Cheddar cheese, shredded | ¾ cup Biscuit mix |
| 1 (4 ounce) can green chiles, | 1¾ cups milk |
|   drained | ½ teaspoon salt |
| 1 bunch green onions, chopped | ½ teaspoon oregano |

Grease a 9-inch pie plate. Place olives, cheese, chiles and onions in pie plate. Combine eggs, biscuit mix, milk, salt and oregano in blender or food processor. Blend for 15 seconds on high speed. Pour gently over the ingredients in pie plate. Bake in 400 degree oven for 25-30 minutes. Serve with salsa or picante sauce.

Yield: 6 servings

## APPLE FLAUTAS

*This delicious fruit/tortilla dish provides a sweet touch to the zesty South of the Border Eggs, while carrying out the Southwest theme beautifully.*

| | |
|---|---|
| 1 pkg. medium flour tortillas | ¼ cup brown sugar |
| 1 large can apple pie filling | Scant cinnamon and nutmeg |

Lay tortilla on a cookie sheet; place about four tablespoons apple pie filling down the center and roll up. Repeat with each tortilla. Sprinkle tortilla with brown sugar, cinnamon and nutmeg. Cover tightly with foil and bake in 350 degree oven for about 15 minutes — just until warm. Serve immediately.

Yield: 6 servings

# TRUE SOUTHERN COMFORT - GRITS

*If you think grits are boring and bland, you probably never had properly cooked grits — creamy, smooth and swimming in butter. I call this "succor" food, as it truly soothes body and spirit! I have my daughter Debbie to thank for the Carolina Shrimp Grits. Deb ran across an article featuring several grits recipes in the food section of her local newspaper and immediately thought of her Mama — the family grits lover. Featured in the article was a recipe combining shrimp with hot cheese grits which struck my fancy. After adding a little of "this and that" to the recipe, I prepared the dish for a brunch for twenty-five guests. It drew raves then, and continues to draw raves. At Occasions, we prepared this dish for a baby christening for seventy-five guests and officially named it Carolina Grits, in honor of the newborn baby girl. I soon was receiving letters requesting the recipe. Our biggest challenge was preparing it for a fancy wedding reception brunch for 150 guests. Boring? Bland? I don't think so — I would say grits can be "glitzy"!*

## CAROLINA SHRIMP GRITS

1½ pound medium raw shrimp, peeled and deveined
8 slices lean bacon
2 cups fresh mushrooms, sliced
Black pepper, to taste
1 tablespoon pureed garlic

3 teaspoons fresh squeezed lemon juice
2 dashes Tabasco
1½ cups green onion tops, sliced
One recipe Cheese Grits (follows)

Dice bacon, discarding fatty parts, and fry in large skillet — do not let it get too crisp; drain and set aside. Leave a thin layer of bacon drippings in skillet. When drippings are quite hot, add shrimp and cook fast, stirring, until they are pink. Add mushrooms and saute, stirring frequently, until golden and tender (about 4 minutes). Add pureed garlic and stir. Stir in lemon juice, Tabasco and black pepper. Sprinkle with the green onions and bacon pieces. Spoon hot shrimp mixture over Cheese Grits.

Yield: 6 servings

## CREAMY CHEESE GRITS

*These cheese grits come with a built-in guarantee: You're guaranteed to proclaim them the best you ever tasted. Great for breakfast, brunch, or as a main entree. Great with barbecued ribs — toss in a green bean or squash casserole and you've got yourself a meal!*

| | |
|---|---|
| 4 cups water | ¼ cup milk (approximate) |
| 1 cup Quick Grits | 1 teaspoon Worcestershire |
| Dash salt | 1 teaspoon pureed garlic |
| 2 eggs, well beaten | Dash cayenne pepper |
| 1 stick margarine | ½ pound Velveeta, cubed |

In heavy saucepan, bring water and salt to a boil; pour grits in slowly, stirring. Let cook, stirring constantly until smooth and thick. With wire whisk, blend in beaten eggs, then add all remaining ingredients, blending well over low heat. When cheese has melted and all is well mixed, pour into a lightly-greased 13x9x2 inch baking dish. Top with grated mild cheddar or Velveeta. Bake in 350 degree oven for about 45 minutes, until set.

Yield: 6 servings

## SAUSAGE AND EGG CHEESE GRITS

*This is a beautiful brunch or breakfast dish, plus it's a meal in one!*

| | |
|---|---|
| 1 recipe Cheese Grits | 1 pound pkg. small pork |
| 6 eggs | sausages, in skins |

Prepare Cheese Grits; place in 13x9x2 inch baking dish. Bake in 350 degree oven for 35-40 minutes, until almost set. While grits are baking, simmer small sausages in a skillet until done; drain. Remove grits from the oven and lay sausages in a tic-tac-toe fashion on top, making a little impression. In the center of the crisscross sausages, make indention with large cooking spoon and crack an egg in each indention. Return to oven and bake until eggs are set. Serve with hot biscuits or toast and a plate of fruit.

Yield: 6 servings

# CURRIED FRUIT

*For a perfect fall and winter accompaniment to breakfast dishes, piping hot Curried Fruit fits the bill. It also contributes marvelous flavor and color to holiday meals, lending itself to any meat dish, especially pork. One of the most beautiful presentations I ever prepared was for a Thanksgiving dinner when I served this Curried Fruit in a puff pastry dough. It could easily have graced the cover of Gourmet magazine! This dish is especially wonderful with Cheese Grits and Quiche.*

| | |
|---|---|
| 1 (16 ounce) can pear halves | SAUCE: |
| 1 (16 ounce) can peach halves | ¾ cup light brown sugar |
| 1 cup maraschino cherries | 1 stick margarine |
| 1 (20 ounce) can pineapple chunks | 2 tablespoons cornstarch |
| 2 bananas, sliced | 1½ teaspoons curry powder |

Drain all fruit well. Arrange fruit in a 13x9x2 inch baking dish. Blend sugar, cornstarch, margarine and curry powder together well. Pour over fruit and bake uncovered in a 325 degree oven for one hour.

Yield: 8-10 servings

Tip: For easy, fast preparation, layer a 13x9x2 inch baking dish with drained pineapple slices, place a peach half on top each pineapple slice; top each peach half with a maraschino cherry. Drizzle curry sauce overall and bake. Makes a beautiful presentation on a serving platter lined with lettuce leaves.

*For a simple breakfast treat, place a three-ounce block of cream cheese on individual plates. Top with fresh fruit of your choice, and pour warmed breakfast cream over all. Now, bring on the Egg Omelets, crispy fried slab bacon, Milk Punches, and a New Orleans Jazz Band!*

# HEARTY SAUSAGE BREAD

*This breakfast/brunch bread is wonderful with any brunch menu! It also freezes well.*

1 pound Jimmie Dean sausage
½ cup onion, chopped
¼ cup grated Parmesan
½ cup grated Swiss cheese
1 egg, beaten
½ teaspoon Tabasco
1 teaspoon salt

2 tablespoons green onion tops, chopped
2 cups Bisquick baking mix
¾ cup milk
¼ cup Hellmann's mayonnaise
2 egg yolks, beaten
1 tablespoon water

Brown sausage and one-fourth cup onion; drain well. Add Parmesan and Swiss cheeses, one egg, Tabasco, salt, and green onion tops. Blend together the Bisquick, milk, and mayonnaise and fold into the sausage/cheese mixture. Place batter in greased 10-inch square baking pan. Mix egg yolks and water and brush top of batter. Bake in 400 degree oven for 25-30 minutes or until done. Cut in squares, slather with butter and enjoy!

Yield: 10 servings

# SAUSAGE BISCUIT BITES

*These biscuits are delicious, so easy to make, and they freeze beautifully.*

¾ pound Jimmie Dean sausage
2¼ cups Bisquick baking mix

²/₃ cup milk
¼ cup butter, melted

Cook sausage until browned, stirring to crumble; drain well and set aside to cool. Blend baking mix, drained sausage and milk only until mixture is moistened — do not overbeat. Place on lightly floured surface and knead 4-5 times. Roll dough to one-half inch thickness and cut with a 1½ inch biscuit cutter. Place biscuits on an ungreased baking sheet and brush tops with melted butter; bake in 450 degree oven for 10-12 minutes or until golden brown.

Yield: 12-14 biscuits

# STRAWBERRY COFFEE CAKE

*Add flair to your next gathering with this delectable Strawberry Coffee Cake. Or, make up a batch in small pans and give as holiday gifts, along with strawberry cream cheese. This recipe was shared by Betty Mitchell, a neighbor of long ago, who had grown up in her grandfather's bakery where she learned the fine art of baking at an early age. Betty made batches of a variety of breads every week and always sent a loaf over to us — were we ever spoiled! It was around that time that I "turned myself in" to Weight Watchers!*

Batter:
3 cups flour
1 teaspoon baking soda
1 teaspoon salt
2 teaspoons cinnamon
1½ cups sugar

2 (10 ounce) pkg. frozen
   strawberries, thawed
3 eggs, well beaten
1¼ cups oil
1¼ cups pecans, chopped

Sift dry mixture together and set aside. Mix strawberries, eggs, oil and pecans. With electric mixer, blend dry mixture and strawberry mixture together, mixing well.

Filling:
1 (8 ounce) pkg. cream cheese,
   softened
1 egg

1 tablespoon flour
⅓ cup sugar

Blend filling ingredients together well and set aside.

Grease two 9-inch loaf pans with cooking spray. Using two-thirds of the batter, divide it between the two pans. In each pan, place one-half of the cream cheese filling, spreading carefully. Cover with remaining batter. Bake in 350 degree oven for 1 hour, 10 minutes, or until toothpick placed in center comes out clean. (Check after one hour.) Serve with strawberry cream cheese for spreading on cake. Delicious!

Yield: 20-24 slices

# ANGEL BISCUITS

*This biscuit recipe has been around since the sixties and is still popular today. Due to the yeast in the batter, Angel Biscuits are actually a cross between a biscuit and a roll; therefore they enhance both breakfast and dinner menus. This delicious dough will keep in the refrigerator for up to one week. Great to have on hand for company!*

| | |
|---|---|
| 5 cups self-rising flour | 2 pkgs. dry yeast |
| ²/₃ cups shortening | 1 teaspoon soda |
| ½ cup sugar | 2 cups buttermilk |
| ¼ cup warm water | |

Place flour and shortening in mixing bowl — cut in with pastry blender until it resembles coarse crumbs. Add sugar and blend. Add yeast that has been dissolved in warm water. Put soda in buttermilk and add to mixture. Drop by heaping tablespoons on lightly sprayed cookie sheet, or roll out and cut with cookie cutter. Bake in 400 degree oven for 10-12 minutes.

Yield: 3-4 dozen biscuits (approximately)

Tip: If refrigerating dough, place in a lightly sprayed bowl with a tight lid.


# ANGEL CINNAMON ROLLS

| | |
|---|---|
| 1 batch Angel Biscuit Dough | ²/₃ cup sugar or more to taste |
| 1 stick softened margarine | 2-3 tablespoons cinnamon |

Roll out Angel Biscuit dough (above recipe) on floured surface to desired thickness. Spread margarine over dough and sprinkle with sugar and cinnamon. Beginning at long end, firmly roll dough. With sharp, serrated knife, cut in one-half inch pieces and place sides touching on ungreased cookie sheet. Bake in a 400 degree oven for 12-15 minutes, or until golden. For topping: Mix one cup powdered sugar with a few drops milk until spreadable — put on hot-from-the-oven rolls. Delicious!

# PEAR RELISH

*For a guarantee that the Angel Biscuits will be superb, make a batch of this chock-full-of-flavor Pear Relish. Or, if you're so inclined, treat your cocktail party guests to this relish, served with Ritz Crackers. Delicious! This old family recipe is from the files of Inez Odom Parker, mother of Kay Parker Chance, my Editor at Portfolio Magazine. Inez was born in Tullos, Louisiana, but lived most of her life in Central Louisiana, and for many years taught Senior English at Alexandria's Bolton High School. Inez passed away in May of 1997 at 92 after a very happy, productive life — what a delight was this lovely, very caring lady. Now, Inez wasn't simply an exceptional mother and brilliant teacher — she was also a most creative cook. Story has it that there was a wonderful peach and pear orchard on the large farm where her husband Wirt Parker raised cotton, sugar cane, corn, potatoes and cattle. Inez decided early on that since the pear crop was by far the most plentiful, she had best pull out recipes from her files and make her own changes to use this succulent fruit. The result was this marvelous Pear Relish. Thanks, Kay, for sharing a part of your sweet mother with us.*

24 large pears  
12 yellow onions, peeled and  
   chopped fine  
8 green bell peppers, chopped fine  
1 pint prepared mustard  
1 pint vinegar  

1 cup water  
3 cups granulated sugar  
1 tablespoon salt  
1 large jar pimento,  
   sliced and chopped  

Cook all the above ingredients 30 to 40 minutes. Seal in sterilized jars. Serve relish with vegetable dinners or to accompany many meats. Delicious spread on Ritz Crackers.

*For a succulent spread for hot breakfast biscuits,*  
*mix orange marmalade with Grand Marnier Liqueur*  
*and a pinch of dry mustard.*

*Danny Allen (Tripp) Daniel, III*

# Sweets

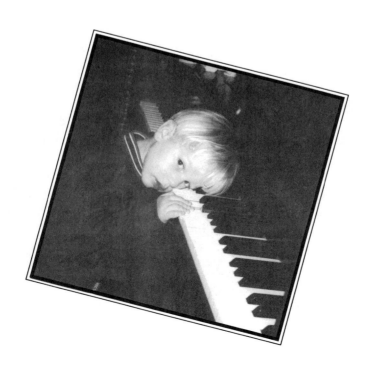

It is important that I preface this chapter by stating that I do not enjoy preparing desserts. I don't mind making an occasional cake because that's a fairly simple procedure, but the idea of doing anything fancier puts me in a tizzy!

People who "work" with dough and do all sorts of magical things with it have my respect. I once asked one of my cooks in the catering business, "how do you knead dough!" You should have seen his face! I have no desire to "work" with dough, whether it be bread dough or pie dough. There is no yearning in me to make my own bread, patiently watching it "rise", although I do, however, own a lovely bread machine which does all these tricks for me.

It's wonderful to live in an age with all the magical appliances to make baking easy. In the old days a cook was equipped with only a spoon, a whisk, a bowl and a stove. In my opinion the convenience of a mix is always appreciated by the busy homemaker. "Made from scratch" is great, but it should be a *choice*, not a *chore*. The bottom line on any dish is "taste" — who cares how it originated? If you can get the same results beginning with a mix, go for it!

My repertoire of recipes for sweets is not large, but I promise you that the cakes, pies, puddings, and other desserts you find in this chapter are all very delicious, especially The Best Bread Pudding In The South, the To-Die-For Banana Pudding, and the Coconut Delight (all featured).

So, when you get a little weary of *kneading, shaping,* and *coddling,* remember it doesn't matter the origin, it's the outcome that counts!

# NEL'S CREME BRULEE'

*My friend, Nel Chavanne made this recipe for very special occasions — holidays, birthdays, and other celebrations. On our birthdays, we eagerly awaited dessert, knowing that Nel had prepared this glorious, wonderful treat for our special day. Nel passed away in May, 1996 following a courageous battle with cancer. A few months before her death, she dropped by my home, carrying a large shopping bag. Out of that bag she pulled a lovely party dress which she knew I had enjoyed borrowing for special occasions, along with the recipe for Creme Brulee'. She quietly said, "why don't you keep this stuff for awhile?" No further words were necessary — we both understood that she wouldn't be with us much longer. That day will linger in my memory for always! On our birthdays we still enjoy Creme Brulee', but somehow, it's just not the same.*

Day before serving:
4 eggs
1 pint heavy cream
4 tablespoons sugar

Dash salt
1½ teaspoons vanilla

Crack and separate eggs. Place yolk in mixing bowl and beat well; set aside. Heat heavy cream and sugar in microwave for twenty seconds, to dissolve sugar. Pour mixture into egg yolks. Beat gently with a whisk — do not bruise eggs. Add salt and vanilla. Pour into individual baking dishes or custard cups. Place baking dishes in a 13x9 inch roaster pan and add water to halfway up sides of dishes. Bake in 300 degree oven for 40 minutes. Bake until custard jiggles a little; remove from oven and cool. Cover and refrigerate.

Day of serving:
Sprinkle a fine layer of brown sugar over the top of the custard. Place in 13x9x2 inch pan again with no water. Place under oven broiler. Custard must be watched carefully — just leave under broiler long enough to melt the sugar. When it cools, sugar hardens. Refrigerate until ready to serve.

Note: Do not cover in refrigerator or topping will become soggy.

Yield: 6 servings

# THE BEST BREAD PUDDING IN THE SOUTH

*This wonderful bread pudding is the best I have ever tasted. Resembling large cinnamon rolls, the presentation of this succulent dessert is met with oohs and aahs! The French bread gives it a bold texture — no soggy mess here! For years I believed my Grandma Jumel was the originator of this dish, only to be told by my cousin Wanda Persac Annison that the creator of this southern favorite was Aunt Linnie Persac, a wonderful lady from my hometown of Baton Rouge whom we all loved and admired. What's important is that it WAS shared and I am grateful!*

| | |
|---|---|
| 1 stick butter or margarine | 1 tablespoon vanilla |
| 1 cup sugar | ½ to ⅔ large loaf |
| 3 eggs | crusty French bread |
| 1 (13 ounce) can evaporated milk | Cinnamon and sugar, to taste |
| 1 can water | ½ cup raisins |

In large bowl cream softened butter and sugar with electric mixer. Add eggs and mix till light and fluffy. Add milk, water, and vanilla. Mix well and stir in raisins. Place in 13x9x2 inch baking dish. Cut French bread in two-inch slices and place in mixture in baking dish, sides touching. Allow one side to absorb liquid, turn over, and let other side absorb juice. Sprinkle top with cinnamon and sugar and bake in a 400 degree oven for 20 minutes or until fluffy and golden-brown. Serve with whiskey sauce.

Note: No matter how well you blend this butter/milk mixture, the butter may "clog" up, due to the cold milk. When you turn over the bread slices, be sure to pick up some of the butter — simply "smear" it on top of bread before you sprinkle the cinnamon/sugar on top.

Whiskey Sauce:

| | |
|---|---|
| ½ cup sugar | 2 tablespoons butter |
| ¼ cup water | 1-2 jiggers whiskey |

Cook first three ingredients in saucepan until dissolved. Remove from heat and add whiskey. Serve hot with bread pudding.

Yield:  10-12 servings

# TO-DIE-FOR BANANA PUDDING

*After years and years of making the same boring banana pudding, I received this recipe from my cousin Deryl McGrew Hamilton of Baton Rouge. It took only one taste of Deryl's recipe for me to know that it was "out" with the old recipe, and "in" with the new one. Deryl and I have shared our love of food since we were kids stealing oysters from Mom's cornbread dressing and terrorizing the elderly aunts when they came to visit. One year apart in age, we were definitely the family "monsters", getting into mischief every chance we had. We're grown up now but our love of entertaining and cooking remains a strong bond between us. Thanks go to Deryl for many memories — both happy and sad. Deryl lost her son, Johnny in a drowning accident in the fall of 1998 — his wonderful smile and ready wit will always be remembered.*

| | |
|---|---|
| 1 large instant vanilla pudding | 2 cups homogenized milk |
| 1 can condensed milk | 1 (12 ounce) Cool Whip |
| 1 pound bag vanilla wafers | 6-7 ripe bananas |

Thaw Cool Whip. Mix pudding, condensed milk, homogenized milk, and three-fourths of the Cool Whip. With electric mixer on medium speed, blend mixture together for about 3 minutes. In a large glass bowl, layer one-third pudding, wafers, and sliced bananas; repeat layers, ending with pudding. Top with reserved Cool Whip. Refrigerate.

Yield: 10-12 servings

*For a simple, elegant dessert, place a large scoop of vanilla ice cream in a pretty crystal dish. Drizzle with Chambord (raspberry liqueur) and sprinkle one tablespoon fresh or frozen raspberries on top. Garnish with one pirouette cookie and a sprig of fresh mint. Easy to prepare, and simply delicious!*

# COCONUT DELIGHT

*Let me preface this recipe with "I hate coconut — always have, always will." I normally won't even taste anything that contains coconut; therefore, it is a mystery that I was prompted into sampling this dessert. I'm so glad I did because it is now one of my favorite desserts. I must confess, however, that I cut down considerably the amount of coconut from the original recipe. This is a beautiful, delicious company dish, guaranteed to end your meal on a festive note!*

| | |
|---|---|
| 1 stick margarine | 1 cup powdered sugar |
| 1 cup flour | 1 can Angel Flake coconut, divided |
| 1¼ cups chopped pecans | 2 small pkgs. instant vanilla pudding |
| 1 (8 ounce) pkg. cream cheese | 3 cups homogenized milk |
| 1 (5 ounce) pkg. Cool Whip | 1 (8 ounce) Cool Whip |

First Layer: Cream margarine and flour until crumbly. Blend in pecans. Place in 13x9x2 inch baking dish and press down to cover bottom. Bake in 350 degree oven for 20 minutes.

Second Layer: Blend together cream cheese, 5 ounce Cool Whip, powdered sugar, one-half can coconut. Spread over cooled first layer.

Third Layer: Mix pudding and milk. Beat on medium speed until pudding thickens and spread over second layer.

Fourth Layer: Top with 8 ounce Cool Whip and sprinkle lightly with coconut. Chill.

Yield: 10-12 servings

## BANANA SPLIT DESSERT

2 cups vanilla wafer crumbs
2 sticks margarine, divided
1 pound powdered sugar
2 eggs
6 ripe bananas

2 (15 ounce) cans crushed
  pineapple, drained well
1 (12 ounce) Cool Whip, thawed
1 cup chopped pecans
1 (10 ounce) jar maraschino
  cherries, chopped

Mix vanilla wafer crumbs with 1 stick melted margarine; place in 13x9x2 inch baking dish and press down to cover bottom. Mix powdered sugar, 2 beaten eggs and 1 stick softened margarine on high speed for 10 minutes. Spread carefully over crust. Split six bananas lengthwise and place over cream filling. On top of bananas, spread drained pineapple. Spread Cool Whip evenly over pineapple layer. Sprinkle with pecans and top that with chopped cherries. Chill; cut in squares to serve.

Yield: 12 servings

## LIGHT AND EASY KAHLUA CHEESECAKE

10 chocolate wafers, finely crushed
1½ cups light cream cheese
1 cup sugar
1 cup small curd cottage cheese
¼ cup + 2 tablespoons cocoa
¼ cup flour

¼ cup Kahlua liqueur
1 teaspoon vanilla
¼ teaspoon salt
1 egg
2 tablespoons chocolate chips

Sprinkle crushed chocolate wafer crumbs in bottom of 7-inch springform pan; set aside. Position knife blade in food processor; add cream cheese and next seven ingredients, processing until smooth. Add egg and process just until blended. Slowly pour mixture over crumbs in pan. Bake in 300 degree oven for 65-70 minutes or until cheesecake is set. Let cool in pan or a wire rack. Cover and chill 8 hours. Remove sides of pan and serve.

Yield: 12 servings

## KIT PARKER'S FRESH APPLE CAKE

*This scrumptious made-from-scratch cake is from the files of the late Inez "Kit" Parker, mother of Kay Chance, my Editor at Portfolio Magazine. This lady was a teacher, a scholar, and a fabulous cook as well.*

1¼ cups Wesson Oil
2 cups granulated sugar
Pinch of salt
2 eggs, well beaten
2 teaspoons vanilla
1½ teaspoons soda

3 cups all-purpose flour
1 teaspoon cinnamon
1 teaspoon nutmeg
3 cups apples, chopped
1 cup pecans, chopped

Mix dry ingredients together. Blend oil, vanilla and eggs. Add chopped apples and pecans. This makes a stiff batter. Bake in a Bundt pan in a 350 degree oven for about 1 hour. Do not grease or line pan.

Yield: 12-14 servings

## CHOCOLATE CHIP POUND CAKE

*Kids love this cake served with vanilla ice cream, but it is also fit for your fanciest guest, served with a dollop of whipped cream and chocolate curls! Thanks for this recipe go to my fun-loving cousin Wanda Persac Annison from Jackson, Mississippi. I have never visited Wanda without returning home with a recipe for something special.*

1 Duncan Hines Yellow Cake Mix
1 (6 ounce) instant chocolate
   pudding
½ cup oil
½ cup water
4 eggs

1 (8 ounce) sour cream
1 (6 ounce) pkg. semi-sweet
   chocolate chips
Whipped cream for topping
   (optional)
Chocolate curls (optional)

Mix together first 6 ingredients in order shown; stir in chocolate chips. Bake in 350 degree oven for 1 hour in a greased Bundt or angel food pan. Remove from oven; let sit 10 minutes and remove from pan to cake plate. Top with dollop of whipped cream and chocolate curls.

Yield: 16 servings

# PERFECT PECAN PIE

*To fully describe my friend Chet Beckwith would take far more than one page of this book! A native of Texas, Chet arrived in my hometown, Baton Rouge, in the fifties to manage Goldrings; several years later he opened his own popular, trend-setting boutique, Chebeck. It wasn't until after retirement that Chet had time to indulge his "other" passion which is cooking, and he went on to make a name for himself as a gourmet chef, not as a business, but as a beloved hobby. To receive an invitation to dine with Chet and his charming wife, Margaret Jo, is considered quite an honor. Chet writes the food and entertainment column entitled "Too Good To Be True" for InRegister, Baton Rouge's popular social magazine, and has written a cookbook by the same title, now in its fourth printing. You don't have to be a cook to enjoy Chet's book — his narrative alone is worth reading. His descriptions are riotous — "prepare to die, it is so good", or "people faint when they taste this dish" or "gravy so good, you'll want to comb it through your hair." Some of Chet's recipes from Too Good To Be True are featured in the hot-off-the-press Best of the Best of Louisiana, Volume II Cookbook. I was proud when Chet featured a couple of my recipes in his cookbook and am equally proud to return the compliment. To quote Chet: "pecan pies may come and go but this one will go on forever. It is not only easy to prepare, but also prize winning good."*

| | |
|---|---|
| 1 cup sugar | 1 cup white Karo syrup |
| 1 "pat" butter | 1 cup pecans, chopped or whole |
| 3 eggs | 1 "running over" teaspoon vanilla |

Cut butter into sugar with pastry blender. Add beaten eggs. Add white Karo syrup, pecans, and vanilla. Mix well. Pour into unbaked pie shell. Bake in preheated, 350 degree oven for 50-55 minutes. Recipe can be easily doubled to make two pies at a time.

Yield: 6 to 8 slices per pie

Tip: Place in 4 mini-sized pie crusts for great gift giving.

# MANDARIN ORANGE CAKE

1 Duncan Hines Yellow Cake Mix
1 can mandarin oranges, undrained
4 eggs
½ cup oil
1 (8 ounce) Cool Whip, thawed

1 (3½ ounce) Jello Vanilla Instant
   Pudding
1 (14 oz.) can crushed pineapple,
   undrained

Place first 4 ingredients in mixing bowl, blend together, and beat with electric mixer at medium speed for 2 minutes. Pour batter into two 9-inch cake pans that have been sprayed well with cooking spray. Bake in 350 degree oven for 30 minutes or until done. After 10 minutes, remove from pans and place on racks to cool. Mix together Cool Whip, pudding and crushed pineapple, with juice and spread on cooled cake. Store cake in refrigerator.

Yield:  16-18 servings

# ED'S APRICOT POUND CAKE

*We serve this pound cake often when we have dinner guests — it's served hot and is absolutely succulent! Try it for your next small dinner party. It is very simple to assemble — pudding can be kept warm and cake can be sliced and ready to pop in oven.*

1 frozen butter pound cake, thawed
1 (5½ ounce) regular vanilla
   pudding (not instant)

1 (16 ounce) can apricot halves
4 tablespoons margarine

Drain apricot halves well; set aside. Prepare pudding, using directions on package — cook until thick. Keep warm. Cut drained apricot halves in half again. Add to pudding. Keep warm. When ready to serve, slice pound cake into 1-inch thick slices; butter lightly. Place cake in oven and heat only until butter is melted and cake is warm. Caution: do not leave in oven too long. Serve with apricot pudding drizzled over warm cake. Serve immediately.

Yield:  6 servings

## AUNT VU'S LEMON MERINGUE PIE

*Aunt Verdith "Vu" Parker, who passed away twelve years ago, was not only my godmother and favorite relative, but was the best cook in our family. Her seafood dishes were legendary! She taught me to make this pie as a young bride and it still remains my favorite lemon pie; it's neither too sweet nor too tart.*

3 eggs, separated
1 (14 ounce) can condensed milk
½ cup lemon juice
1 teaspoon grated lemon rind

1 graham cracker crust
¼ teaspoon cream of tarter
$^1/_3$ cup sugar

In medium bowl, beat egg yolks. Stir in condensed milk, lemon juice, and rind. Pour into crust. In small bowl, beat egg whites with cream of tarter until foamy; gradually add sugar, beating until stiff but not dry. Spread meringue on top of pie, sealing carefully to edge of crust. Bake in 350 degree oven for 15 minutes or until meringue is golden brown. Cool.

Yield: 8 servings

## KEY LIME PIE

1 (9-inch) baked pastry shell,
    cooled
4 eggs, separated
1 (14 ounce) can condensed milk

½ cup Key lime juice
Few drops green food coloring
½ teaspoon cream of tartar
$^1/_3$ cup sugar

In medium bowl, beat egg yolks. Stir in condensed milk, Key lime and food coloring. In small bowl, stiffly beat 1 egg white; fold into condensed milk mixture. Put in baked pie shell. For meringue, beat remaining 3 egg whites with cream of tartar until foamy. Gradually beat in sugar, beating until stiff but not dry. Spread meringue on top of pie, sealing carefully to edge of shell. Bake in 350 degree oven for 15 minutes or until meringue is golden brown. Refrigerate.

Yield: 8 servings

# GERMAN CHOCOLATE PIE

| | |
|---|---|
| ⅓ cup brown sugar | 1 unbaked pie shell |
| ⅓ cup margarine | 1 bar German chocolate |
| ⅓ cup coconut | 1 large pkg. regular vanilla |
| ½ cup chopped pecans | pudding, <u>not instant</u> |

Melt margarine and blend in brown sugar, coconut, and pecans. Spread in unbaked pie shell. Bake pie shell in 375 degree oven for 10 minutes, or until golden. Cook vanilla pudding with finely chopped German chocolate until chocolate is melted, stirring constantly to avoid pudding sticking and burning on the bottom. Simmer until pudding reaches a boil on low-to-medium heat. Remove from stove and allow to cool five minutes, stirring twice. Pour into pie shell and chill. Serve with dollop of whipped cream.

Yield: 8 servings

# PRALINE PUMPKIN PIE

*As with the German Chocolate Pie, the succulent crust is the secret!*

| | |
|---|---|
| 1 (9-inch) pie shell | 3 eggs, slightly beaten |
| 3 tablespoons margarine | 1½ cups pumpkin |
| ⅓ cup brown sugar | ½ cup white sugar |
| ⅓ cup chopped pecans | ½ cup brown sugar |
| 1 cup evaporated milk | 1 teaspoon salt |
| ½ cup water | 1½ tablespoon pumpkin spice |

Cream margarine, ⅓ cup brown sugar and pecans. Press in bottom of unbaked pie shell. Bake in 450 degree oven for 10 minutes. Combine milk and water and scald in heavy saucepan; set aside. Mix together all remaining ingredients and blend well; beat in scalded milk and water and pour in pie shell. Bake in 350 degree oven for 50 minutes. To serve, top with whipped cream.

Yield: 8 servings

# DIVINE CHOCOLATE/BERRY PIE

*A profusion of rich, creamy chocolate, teamed up with juicy strawberries combine to make a delectable dessert that will embellish a meal like a silver frame sets off a beautiful picture. Serve this picture-perfect pie for the ultimate touch to your next dinner party. Don't let the somewhat lengthy instructions intimidate you — if I can make it, so can you; believe me, it's worth the effort.*

1¼ cups vanilla wafer
    crumbs, crushed
3 tablespoons sugar
¹/₃ cup butter or margarine, melted
½ cup, plus 2 tablespoons semi-
    sweet chocolate morsels,
    divided

1 (8 ounce) cream cheese, softened
¼ cup firmly packed brown sugar
½ teaspoon vanilla
1 (8 ounce) Cool Whip
1 pint fresh strawberries
1½ - 2 teaspoons margarine

Combine first 3 ingredients, mixing well. Firmly press into bottom and sides of lightly greased 9-inch pie plate. Bake in 325 degree oven for 10 minutes. Cool completely. Place one-half cup semi-sweet morsels in large measuring cup; melt uncovered in microwave, setting timer on 1 minute, stir, 1 minute, stir, etc. Set chocolate aside to cool slightly. Beat cream cheese with electric mixer until light and fluffy. Add brown sugar and vanilla, mixing well. Add cooled chocolate and mix well. Fold Cool Whip into cream cheese mixture. Spoon filling into crust and chill for 6-8 hours. When cold and ready to serve, garnish as follows: Set aside one large strawberry and cut remaining strawberries into thick slices. Arrange slices over filling — start at outside and go to center, overlapping strawberries, in pinwheel fashion. Place a whole berry in the center. Put remaining 2 tablespoons of chocolate morsels and 1½-2 teaspoons margarine into a measuring cup; melt uncovered in microwave. When melted, drizzle lightly over strawberries. Place in refrigerator until time to serve.

Yield: 8 servings

# PECAN DAINTIES

*Many years ago my aunt Blanche Wood gave a patio party in honor of my graduation. She served these delightful praline-like dainties which became the "hit" of the evening. Each guest was thrilled to receive a copy of the recipe, printed out on festive, colorful index cards. At Occasions Catering these treats added pizzazz to our finger dessert trays and were always sure to disappear fast. These delicacies also score high for gift-giving since they keep beautifully in an airtight container.*

2½ cups pecan halves
1 cup light brown sugar
1 tablespoon flour

1 egg white
½ teaspoon salt
1 teaspoon vanilla

Beat egg whites until stiff, standing up in peaks, but not dry. Mix and sift sugar, flour, salt; fold into beaten egg whites. Add vanilla and fold in pecan halves. Drop from a teaspoon 2 pecan halves at a time, well spaced on a well-greased cookie sheet which has first been lined with foil. Bake in 275 degree oven for 25-35 minutes. Remove from oven, cool thoroughly and place in an airtight container.

Yield: 3-4 dozen

Tip: When dropping these on the cookie sheet, the idea is to have the dough clinging to the pecans. The pecans are the focal point, with the dough holding them together. Make them tiny. You'll get the hang of it once you pull the first batch out of the oven.

*For a classic ending to a party, serve steaming hot coffee in delicate china cups. Top with whipped cream and drizzle Creme d'Menthe on top. To delight guests even further, present each with a chocolate-coated spoon wrapped in cellophane and tied with a pretty bow. These gourmet spoons can be purchased in a variety of flavors in gourmet liquor stores.*

# MERINGUE KISSES

*As a caterer, with finger dessert trays in great demand during the holidays, I could not have made it without these melt-in-your-mouth, light and airy little puffs. The only setback was the fact that they simply don't work in a gas oven with a pilot light, since they must remain in the oven for several hours. To solve our problem, during the party season I would make a double batch every night at home and pop them in the electric oven. In the morning I would package up last evening's batch in airtight containers and prepare another double batch to remain in the oven all day. This went on each and every day in December! For a long time, I could not even look at one of these little gems without gagging!*

| | |
|---|---|
| 2 egg whites | 1 teaspoon vanilla |
| ¼ teaspoon salt | 1 cup chocolate chips |
| 1 cup sugar | 1 cup finely chopped pecans |

Preheat oven to 350 degrees. Beat egg whites with salt until stiff. Slowly beat in sugar. Continue beating until very stiff. Fold in vanilla, chocolate chips and nuts. With a teaspoon drop batter on lightly greased cookie sheets in small amounts. When ready to put in the oven, turn the oven off. Place cookie sheets in oven, close oven door and leave in oven overnight or for at least 6 hours. Remove from cookie sheet and store in airtight container.

Yield: 4-5 dozen

Tip: If you are making these for guests and want them snowy white, use white vanilla; also be sure that the oven is off when you put them in. They turn brown very quickly! I had to sacrifice and eat all the brown ones that could not be used for party trays. It was a tough job, but someone had to do it!

Tip: Meringue Kisses are also delicious when butterscotch chips are substituted for the chocolate. Almonds are wonderful in place of the pecans. Use your imagination!

# SNICKERDOODLES

*These cookies are old-time favorites. Makes a heap and the kids love them.*

½ cup shortening
½ cup Fleischmann's margarine
1½ cups sugar
2 eggs
2¾ cups flour

2 teaspoons cream of tartar
1 teaspoon soda
¼ teaspoon salt
2 tablespoons sugar
2 teaspoons cinnamon

Mix shortening and margarine, sugar, and eggs thoroughly. Blend in flour, cream of tartar, soda, and salt, mixing well. Shape dough into 1-inch balls. Roll in a mixture of two tablespoons sugar and two teaspoons cinnamon. Place 2 inches apart on an ungreased baking sheet. In a 350° oven, bake 8 to 10 minutes. These cookies puff up, then flatten out.

Yield: 6 dozen

# MELT-IN-YOUR-MOUTH BROWNIES!

1 (8 ounce) cream cheese, softened
1 egg
1½ cups sugar, divided
1½ teaspoons salt, divided
1 (6 ounce pkg.) chocolate chips
1½ cups flour

¼ cup cocoa
1 teaspoon baking soda
1 cup water
⅓ cup Crisco oil
1 tablespoon white vinegar
1 teaspoon vanilla

Combine cream cheese, egg, one-half cup sugar, one-half teaspoon salt. Mix until completely blended. Stir in chocolate chips; set aside. Combine flour, remaining sugar and salt, cocoa, and soda. In another bowl, stir together water, oil, vinegar, and vanilla. Stir into dry mixture and blend well. Pour batter into ungreased 13x9x2 inch baking dish. Drop cream cheese mixture on top of batter by tablespoons, swirling with knife. Bake in 350 degree oven for 30 minutes or until set. Cool at least 30 minutes before cutting.

Yield: 35-40

# Memories

Angelina Rills Jumel

General Allen Jumel

James Major Jumel & Milda
50th Wedding Anniversary - 1950 (Mom 2nd from left)

Since this book is about tradition and family, I feel it's fitting to include this chapter of memories for the special people in my life.

Grandchildren are such fun, and I'm proud to say that several of mine have shown an early interest in cooking — Justin and Adam with their breakfast dishes and drinks, Jill with her tossed salads and cakes, Alec, with a gourmet dessert especially for kids which was featured in my column when he was five years old, and Courtney with her handprint cookies. Carol Ann and Sara are busy with ballet, tennis, and parties and have not yet spent much time in the kitchen, but next time they visit, we'll give it a whirl. Three-year-old Tripp is indifferent to who does the cooking, so long as there's food!

During my children's early years, they made many treasures for me — an apple studded with cloves made by Debbie at age ten; that same apple is now the size of a plum, but is still proudly displayed on our piano every Christmas! I cherish the delicate angels Donna made many years ago, and as I hang them on the tree each year, I am reminded of that precious little girl who spent so much time making them for her Mom. There's the memorable gift from Danny — the bright blue construction paper where he drew his tiny hand prints and wrote in his faltering first grade handwriting, "I love you, Mom".

This *is* a cookbook, after all, and I would normally mention early cooking skills and eating habits of my kids, but some memories are best forgotten. If I remember correctly, I spoon fed them until they were six, cut their meat until they were fifteen, and served as their short-order cook every day. In order to entice my Donna to eat *anything*, I had to cut her bologna into pinwheels on her plate and surround them with bread which had been cut into pretty little shapes with a cookie cutter. That was the only food she ate until she was 21!

I have a wealth of memories of my children — both the fun and the serious — for they have made me proud every day of their lives. With this book, I give them my memories and family traditions, but most of all, I give them my love.

# Beginnings...

Me, Scotty & Dad

Mom, the flapper

Dad

Scotty, Mom & Me

*My Brother & Me...*

*Big Brother,*
*Little Sister*

*Scotty with*
*Momoo, Dad's Mom*

*My protector*

*July 1968*
*Scotty back from 'Nam*

*May 1997*
*The Bluffs*

# Scotty and Family

Ladye and Scotty with cousins,
Johnny, Deryl and L'Shele Hamilton

Green Beret Days

Mom with Scott White III and Family

John, Naval Aviator
&
Scott III, Black Beret

Mom with John White and Family

Hugging Mom 1993

# Me Me and Family

Me Me with Donna, Me and Jill - 2002

Mom Dancing Class 1967

Me Me with Adam and Debbie - 2002

Justin, #1
Great-Grandson 2002

Mom & Me with Southern Cousins

Me Me & Ed
1993

# Me Me and Family

Danny & Family with Me Me
Easter 1998

A visit with Courtney 1995

Aunt Verdith & Me Me dancing

Ed's Mom, Louise & Me Me
Thanksgiving 1983

Me Me
jitterbugging 1992

Jill, Deb, Me & Me Me - Christmas, 1989

# My Children

*Deb & Donna - 1960*
*Donna's 1st Birthday*

*Danny out-fished them all!*
*Gulf of Mexico - 1973*

*Deb, Danny & Donna - 1981*

*Cheers! 1971*

*Donna, Mom, & Deb - 2001*

# My Children

Deb,
Danny,
& Donna
- 1992

Donna & Deb
1980

Danny, 1 year

Thanksgiving Reunion - 1996

*Grandkids*

Fun in Baton Rouge with
Carol Ann, Sara & Tripp

Courtney's Christening - 1989

Alec, Jill, Ma Maw, Adam, Justin & Carol Ann - 1992

Adam w/Pumpkin Jill
Halloween 1988

Jill & Courtney
Visit - 1995

# Grandkids

Thanksgiving 1996

Sara -2002

Carol Ann 1992

Cousins, Jill & Adam 1993

Fishing fun

Justin & Tripp
Easter 2002

Tripp, Sara, Carol Ann, & Alec - Xmas 2000

Deb & Boys

## Debbie, Randy, Justin & Adam

Christmas in Oklahoma 1998

Justin & Baby Adam
1985

Adam & Justin - 1988

Deb, Randy, & Boys

Denver, Colorado 1990

# Donna, Lee, and Jill

Jill's 2nd Birthday 1990

Mom, Dad, and Jill 1998

Jill, Cheerleader – 9th grade

Thanks Mom!
Jill 1992

Jill and Mom, Thanksgiving 2001

Jill in Ma Maw's jewelry 1993

# Danny, Carol, Alec, Carol Ann, Sara, & Tripp

Easter 1997

Newly Weds - 1988

A family picture 1999
Sage Studio, Baton Rouge, LA

Carol Ann & Alec - 1993

Sara & Tripp visit Me Me - 1998

# Susan, Michael, and Courtney

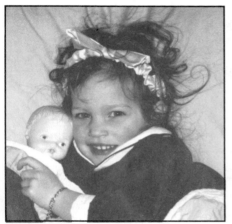

Courtney - 1991

The Czarnecke's, Christmas 1999

Ma Maw & Courtney 2002

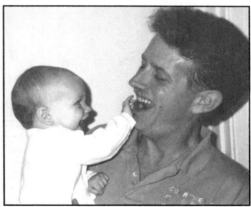

Courtney playing w/Pa Paw

Dad & Courtney, 1 year old

Michael, Louise, Susan, & Ed 1986

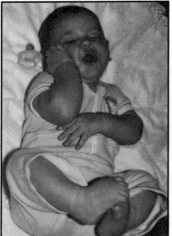

Justin - Pooped Out!

# Visions of Sugarplums

Donna, Deb, & Babies - 1964

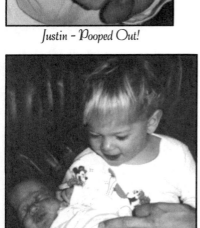

Alec w/New Sister,
Carol Ann - 1991

Danny & Alec
A Long Day Fishing

Sh!
Asleep at Last!

Alec &
Pa Paw
Snoozing

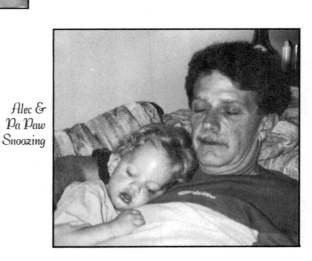

# Visions of Sugarplums

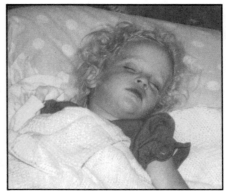

Sara - Our Little Angel

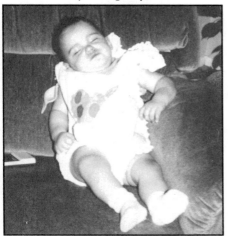

Jill - Do Not Disturb!

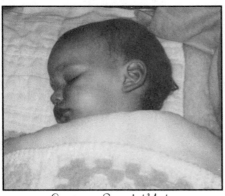

Courtney - Snuggled Under

Tripp - So Good!

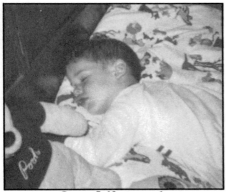

Danny & Pooh - 1967

Adam - Sentry Duty!

# Family Update - 2002

Debbie & Family

Donna & Family

Susan & Family

Danny & Family

May 2000, 20th Anniversay Cruise

...and Charlie

# Index

# $\mathscr{Index}$

# Order Blank

To order *"So Good...Make You Slap Your Mama!"* Simply fill out the form below and return it with your check to:

**Marlyn Monette**
~~**604 Pierremont Road**~~  165 Vidor Lane
**Shreveport, LA ~~71106~~**  71105

Please send _____ copies ...................... @ $16.95 each _____

($4 for 1 book, add $2 for each additional book) Shipping _____

(Louisiana 8¼%) Sales tax _____

**Ship To:**                                              Total _____

Name_____

Address _____

City_____ State_____ Zip _____

Make checks payable to: Marlyn Monette
Phone: 318-868-5804 • Fax: 318-868-9051
E-mail: marlynm4@aol.com • Website: www.slapyourmama.com

- - - - - - - - - - - - - - - - - - - - - - - - - - - - - - - -

# Order Blank

To order *"So Good...Make You Slap Your Mama!"* Simply fill out the form below and return it with your check to:

**Marlyn Monette**
**604 Pierremont Road**
**Shreveport, LA 71106**

Please send _____ copies ...................... @ $16.95 each _____

($4 for 1 book, add $2 for each additional book) Shipping _____

(Louisiana 8¼%) Sales tax _____

**Ship To:**                                              Total _____

Name_____

Address _____

City_____ State_____ Zip _____

Make checks payable to: Marlyn Monette
Phone: 318-868-5804 • Fax: 318-868-9051
E-mail: marlynm4@aol.com • Website: www.slapyourmama.com

*The Times* – Shreveport, Louisiana - Carolyn Flournoy, Food Editor –
June 9, 1999
"Close to home we have a splendid new cookbook, *So Good...*In
this, her first cookbook, she combines family memories with succulent
recipes.

*The Ponca City News* – Ponca City, OK – *The Neighborhood Chef* –
Sherry Muchmore – Tuesday, March 7, 2000
"... and when she (Marlyn) writes, you feel like you're sitting across
the table, with a hot cup of coffee, having a pleasant little chat with your
best friend. I was so taken with this lady's way with words and style, I
just wanted to share her with you. The joy of family and friends reign
supreme as each chapter begins with pictures of members of her family
so dear to her...there are too many good recipes in this cookbook that
once is just not enough to cook with Ms. Monette...

*The Advocate* – Baton Rouge, Louisiana – *Book Report* - Cheramie
Sonnier, Food Editor – August 5, 1999
"...The cookbook is filled with lots of chitchat and another plus is
that the recipes are printed in easy-to-read type.

*Country Roads* – St. Francisville, Louisiana - Dorcus Brown, Publisher –
August, 1999
...The book is a collage of alluring recipes new and old, family
memories and anecdotes from a lifetime's entertaining...*So Good...*
brings all her (Marlyn) experience to bear on over 180 distinctly Southern dishes from Donna's Artichoke Dip to Nonnon Yeagley's Yams. As
the names suggest, many come with stories attached—hints of their
heritage—that add to the volume's double function: as not only a
cookbook, but as a tribute to the friends and family whom Monette has
entertained, and been entertained by, over the years.

***The Times of Acadiana*** – Lafayette, Louisiana – *Feed Me* - Eileen Fontenot – September 22, 1999

"*So Good...*, a cookbook in which she pays homage to great Southern cooking, such as chicken and sausage gumbo, chicken and dumplings, sausage jambalaya, crawfish fettuccini.

***Lake Charles American Press*** – Lake Charles, Louisiana – Dorothy C. Stroud, Life Editor – October 6, 1999

"The book combines family memories, amusing stories and succulent recipes."

***InRegister*** – Baton Rouge, Louisiana – *Too Good To Be True* column – Chet Beckwith, Food Editor

"She (Marlyn) is a caterer, columnist, cookbook author and all sorts of good things."

"Those North Louisiana people, especially if they're originally from South Louisiana—as Marlyn is—certainly know how to lay out a good spread."

***Portfolio Magazine*** – Shreveport, LA – Kay Chance, Publisher/Editor – March, 1999

"A 'must-have' cookbook for those who love good food...this incredible collection of taste-tempting recipes, easy-to-follow and most unique, is laced throughout with family memories, amusing stories and delightful photographs...Marlyn and her cooking expertise have become synonymous in Shreveport...her Occasions Catering remains a very special memory for her many happy clients.